The Game Is Playing Your Kid

THE GAME
IS PLAYING YOUR KID

*How to Unplug and Reconnect
in the Digital Age*

DR. JOE DILLEY

Bascom Hill Publishing Group,
Minneapolis

BASCOM
HILL BOOKS

Bascom Hill Publishing Group
322 First Avenue N, 5th floor
Minneapolis, MN 55401
612.455.2294
www.bascomhillbooks.com

The stories in this book are based on true experiences and have been edited to remove identifying information to protect confidentiality. This book is not intended to substitute for professional treatment, but to be used as a guide to effective parenting with regard to electronics use. The book can thus also be used to augment professional treatment. The specific circumstances, conditions, relationships, past experiences, and a plurality of other factors can differ substantially between one individual and another and could affect or lead to changes in treatments and/or diagnoses, and such varying factors with relation to the reader may cause the appropriate treatment for a particular reader to differ from the approaches described in this book. As a result, I strongly suggest seeking individualized treatment, particularly if you or someone you know is struggling with acute problems.

ISBN-13: 978-1-63413-296-1
LCCN: 2015900022

Distributed by Itasca Books

Cover Design by Jake Dilley
Typeset by Sophie Chi

Printed in the United States of America

Praise for *The Game Is Playing Your Kid: How to Unplug and Reconnect in the Digital Age*:

"Dr. Dilley's clinical expertise and pragmatic style shine through in this timely antidote to today's screen problem. This book should be mandatory reading for anyone raising a child in today's high tech world."

—Stephanie N. Marcy, PhD, Assistant Professor of Clinical Pediatrics, USC Keck School of Medicine

"Are you a parent who is tired of screen time battles? Do you wonder how to help your kids and your family unplug at least some of the time in order to find real connection in the digital age? With wisdom, humor and compassion, Dr. Joe Dilley shares practical tools that will help you make things different for you, your kids, and your family. Read *The Game is Playing Your Kid*!"

—Melissa J. Johnson, PhD, Psychologist, Founder and CEO of the Institute for Girls' Development

"At last – guidance for parents trying to navigate parenting a child in the electronic age! *The Game is Playing Your Kid* provides a practical, family centered guide to helping young people create a balanced life that includes recreational electronics. Most importantly, *The Game is Playing Your Kid* encourages a collaborative problem solving approach between parent and child when there is conflict around issues of electronics use. This book will be helpful as well to professionals working with families who struggle with issues of electronics use."

—Diane Danis, MD, MPH, Developmental and Behavioral Pediatrician

"Dr. Dilley has tackled one of the major stresses of present day parenting (how do we manage our children's use of electronic media). It certainly takes evaluating our own behavior with media and refining parenting skills. Even though parenting requires constant challenges, the uniqueness of electronic gaming has elevated that demand. Dr. Dilley has provided tools for parents to reestablish operational control."

—Leonard R. Baker III, MD, Co-director Descanso Medical Center for Development and Learning, Clinical Professor of Pediatrics, USC Keck School of Medicine

"*The Game is Playing Your Kid* tackles one of the biggest problems facing parents in the technology age . . . screen time. Dr. Dilley brings awareness and healthy responses to many issues facing families, when electronic devices become idols in kids' lives. Dr. Dilley relays stories that every parent can relate to, and offers pragmatic solutions that are sometimes hard for us to see when we are on the inside looking out."

—Justin Hartwig, Super Bowl Champion, Certified Health Coach, and Proud Father

"In an age where even the most revered professionals are polarized on the topic of technology, Dr. Dilley presents an even-handed approach to the screen time dilemma, one rooted in a fundamental understanding of human drives and our need for connection. This book is a must-read for anyone with children or anyone who wonders if they use technology or technology uses them.

Dr. Dilley deeply understands the screen-time dilemma and effortlessly weaves together personal experience with professional research to present a coherent, entertaining, and essential resource for anyone with children or adolescents. His stories reveal a dimension of Joe's personality that enlightens, entertains, and validates the experience of those trying to serve adolescents and their frustrated parents.

I never thought parenting advice could be so rich, shocking, and hilarious as the stories I found within this book. Dr. Dilley's confident yet self-effacing demeanor makes him the perfect man to write a book about many challenging obstacles familiar to most every parent.

The screen time dilemma is raised by every parent in my practice—from parents of toddlers to parents of teens—and I'm happy to recommend Dr. Dilley's book as a resource to help them navigate these treacherous waters. His practical interventions ascend to the level of hypothetical scripts for conversations you may have one day. This is an essential resource I will use as both a psychologist and a parent."

—Ryan Howes, PhD, ABPP

- Board Certified clinical psychologist in private practice
- Clinical Professor of Psychology, Fuller School of Psychology
- Founder, National Psychotherapy Day
- Blogger, *Psychology Today*
- Columnist, *Psychotherapy Networker* Magazine

*To my magnificent daughter
and her entire generation.*

May your character always play the Game.

Contents

STEP III: Tailor the Solution to Fit Your Family's Needs and Values

Introduction

You want your child to listen to you when you ask him to turn off the game, phone, or tablet. Better grades are a high priority of yours, too. And while you want your children to enjoy being kids, it troubles you that they prefer screen-based activity to almost everything else. You can't believe it, but it's become a bedtime battle to get the electronic devices powered down and put away. You're fatigued by how the battle repeats itself during the morning routine before everyone goes their separate ways for a busy day. Ugh.

I get it.

This book details a simple but powerful three-step process designed to eliminate any overreliance on, or misuse of, technology occurring in your home. I use the process and pass it along to parents regularly in my private psychology practice, where I've helped hundreds of families over the past ten years address their screen problem. In fact, the process is so effective that I have developed a love for implementing it to help families unplug from electronic devices, and reconnect with one another in more organic and lasting ways. How great does it sound to scoop up all the energy you presently spend on arguing, and deposit it instead into times of authentic and mutual enjoyment that bring you closer to one another? That would be nice, wouldn't it?

Does that scenario sound too good to be true? Maybe it is.

Or maybe . . . you know that such a scenario is possible and that you just need help getting there. Maybe you've had enough. You're ready to make a change. Maybe you're excited at the idea of declaring *Game Over* on having to beg your child to turn off the device and study. If so, then let's play a new game. I'll be the coach and guide you through the three steps of the game, the object of which is to liberate your child from being played and have him reclaim the title of *Game Player*.

STEP I:

Become the Expert on Your Family's Screen Problem

Chapter 1

Placing the Problem in Context

"The water is inside the fish, but the fish is also inside the water."

—*Unknown*

As a clinical psychologist, I feel privileged to help individuals and families address a lot of very serious issues. Because my private practice is located within a fairly affluent area of Greater Los Angeles, I also hear a lot of good problems. Good problems are setbacks that most of us would consider relatively benign in the scheme of things, like having a BMW break down or "suffering" through a vacation with the extended family. These are "problems," but encountering them in the first place requires considerable good fortune as a prerequisite.

The Electronics Addiction: A Good Problem

The electronics addiction is the most common good problem that comes through my office door these days. In many homes, technology meant to illuminate the mind ends up only illuminating the living room. Incredulous parents bring their children and adolescents to my office, asking how to unplug them from their screens without unplugging the family's technology altogether. After all, how do you keep Junior off the Internet when he knows more about how to connect to it than you do? Hmmm. It really is a problem, albeit one only encountered by those of us fortunate enough to possess these kinds of technologies in our homes.

This book's strategies are built on the idea that technology is a modern-day privilege for those of us fortunate enough to have it; it is not a universal "given." As we discuss these strategies, I encourage you to consider not only their positive effects within your home, but also how your family's healthier living will inspire other families. At a societal level, the electronics addiction isn't a good problem at all. We live during a time in which some shoppers shiver all Thanksgiving night only to trample one another to death in a sunrise race through the electronics store to buy gaming consoles that allow them to create avatars of themselves. And some drivers risk killing themselves or others to send a text instead of simply pulling over first.

What a lousy game we play when we risk our lives for the sake of the screen. I'm glad you've decided to join me in playing a new game.

Spelunking

It takes remarkable courage to initiate the process of individual or family psychotherapy: Making change, even for the better, is *hard*. Therapy comes with costs in terms of time and money, and we are socialized into believing that if we seek therapy, we must be "crazy." We ask, "What's the matter with me?" or "What's the problem inside my child?" These questions elicit feelings of shame because they place the person asking them at the center of the problem.

Instead, I suggest we think about psychotherapy with a smile by taking a lead from our friends in the dentistry profession. Nobody feels ashamed of going to the dentist; it's socially appropriate to take care of your teeth, even preventively. In short, it's more normal to take care of our *dental* health than our *mental* health . . . it's more acceptable to care for our mouths than our minds. I'd like to shake up that conventional thinking and suggest that proactive care for all parts of our being, especially our relationships with self and other, is essential— and it does not require there to be something "wrong" with a patient.

In my practice, I do not let parents drop off their kids for repair, simply because I know the children are not the problem (even when their behavior is problematic), so such an approach will not be helpful. Fixing the parents is not the solution either, for the same reason. My job is not to fix people, but to help whole families improve their home environments. That means parents are integral to the solution, so I want them to attend the therapy sessions with their kids.

During one family's first therapy session with me, the father chuckled in disbelief as he recounted several instances of catching his nine-year-old son "spelunking" around the house. The father explained that his son had recently established a practice of setting an alarm clock for the middle of the night, waking himself up, and tiptoeing around in the dark until he found an accessible electronic device, like his father's tablet or his mother's smartphone. The boy played with whichever device(s) he found, sometimes until daybreak. As you might imagine, his school performance was suffering.

During the session, I determined that the boy was feeling shortchanged by his parents, who had recently begun limiting his use of electronics because they found his gaming to be excessive. In response, the boy created his clandestine nightly ritual to compensate for any screen time he had "missed out on" during the preceding day. The parents sought my counsel to fix the problem— but exactly what was the problem? Was the boy "hooked" on electronics? Or was spelunking a creative way of disregarding a strict rule?

As was the case for this family, managing your family's screen time and making sure your child is playing the game—without being played by it— begins with becoming the expert on the problem.

The Fruity Button

As I completed my doctorate in clinical psychology, I interned at a children's clinic in Los Angeles whose training director used a framework called Family Systems to make sense of family problems and identify solutions to those problems. A Family Systems framework suggests that family problems are just that: problems within families. Kids will necessarily act out as their brains and bodies mature, and the environment will necessarily influence and be influenced by those processes of maturation. So too, while each of us has innate strengths and weaknesses that inevitably impact the world around us, we are in turn impacted by that world. As you can imagine, good family therapy uses this framework to solve many family problems. Let's implement it here to place your family's screen problem in its proper context.

Imagine for a moment that every time you pushed a button, your brain released a chemical that brought you a little dose of pleasure. Understandably, you would feel tempted to continue to push the button. The button is the proverbial forbidden fruit.

Now imagine that the button says *ON* or *POWER*, and that it tantalizes your index finger from its fixed position on a computer, tablet, smartphone, or gaming system. When you push the button, a most appealing chain reaction occurs. Colorful characters appear, music plays, virtual friends surround you—you are immediately and completely sucked into a different world, where all the control you lacked throughout your workday is now located at your fingertips.

Or maybe your system doesn't require a handheld controller at all. One of my favorite movies, *Back to the Future Part II*, accurately predicts present-day reality in a scene when two young characters from the future complain that having to "use your hands" to play a video game renders the game "a baby's toy." Indeed, if you own such a gaming system, all you need to do is position your body to control your on-screen character—no hand controller required. And your on-screen avatar looks just like you; you created it to look like that. No wonder some of these characters are named Mii.

As you immerse yourself in this narcissistic fantasy world, the chemical being released in your brain is called dopamine, and you are hardwired to find its release pleasurable. The fact that you enjoy the dopaminergic release, and thus prefer pushing the button to pushing the pencil, is certainly not your "fault."

Now imagine you are told, without any warning (from your perspective), that you are no longer allowed to play the game until a seemingly arbitrary period of time has passed. Under these new conditions, what do you have to look forward to each morning? Another long day at an unpaid job, where your boss talks a lot and you have to take notes on what she says—before she sends you home with even more work to do. In this context, it's understandable that you might wake yourself up at 3:00 AM for some dopamine-inducing spelunking that feels especially thrilling because of the adrenaline it releases, since you do it in secret. While spelunking constitutes problematic behavior, it actually makes sense, given your circumstances.

Stepping out of that thought exercise, it's clear that your child is not the problem. Rather, he is human. Spelunking is what we all are inclined to do when we feel shortchanged on our pleasure: We start seeking it in unhealthy ways that come at a cost. In short, we start to be owned by our desires or belongings, instead of owning them.

Let's contemplate your family's screen problem by way of an additional paradigm, one that you, yourself, might have encountered in real life. You might have noticed how difficult it can be to pull yourself away from a slot machine. My very first psychology professor in college observed, "If you want to see rats pressing a food bar over and over again until a pellet of food is dispensed, you don't need to come to my lab. Go to a casino and watch people mindlessly pulling the levers of slot machines." People get addicted to slots because until and unless you hit the jackpot, you receive a pellet of reward every once in a while. The machine pays you a little teaser to keep you playing. Or does the machine pay to keep playing *you*? In the end, doesn't the house always win?

That's exactly what happens with kids and video games: kids get played by video games. If they stop playing, their progress is lost, their characters "die," and their online friends are disappointed. If they continue playing, the games reward them by "unlocking" new features and awarding valuable virtual commodities. The games even reward them if they're not very good gamers. Many of today's games are engineered to go on forever. So while older gamers remember losing interest when they repeatedly lost a game, younger gamers feel like they win even when they lose, so they keep playing. Kids' behaviors and temperaments start to hinge directly on their access to these games and "how far they get" in them. There is no question who the players are and who is getting "gamed."

Game and app developers have figured out how to put all the bells and whistles of the casino right into gamers' homes, and even into their pockets. I bet my first psychology professor now suggests his students enter a restaurant and watch diners sitting together vegging out—not with what's on their plates, but with what's on their phones.

So if your kid isn't the problem, does that mean that you, the parent, are the problem after all?

No.

You didn't choose for things to be this way. You love your son and gave him the Xbox as a birthday gift, not realizing he would play it instead of sleeping. You graciously passed along your old phone without any idea that your daughter would figure out how to connect it to Wi-Fi and post an inappropriate selfie on a social-media profile.

The Fishbowl Ecosystem

The essence of Family Systems thinking is captured by the quote that opened this chapter: "The water is inside the fish, but the fish is also inside the water." In a fishbowl, no fish is a passive participant in the fishbowl's ecosystem, so the same is true for your family and your environment. Along with your child, you are also a fish who necessarily ingests, expels, and exists in the water filling your bowl.

And if the water becomes polluted, then *all* the fish take in the polluted water. A polluted bowl doesn't support thriving for its individual members or the group as a unit. Now *there* is the problem. The members and the group share this communal problem.

The drama resulting from your family's screen problem is the pollution permeating your fishbowl. Because you are an active participant in your ecosystem, you are both complicit in its pollution, yet capable of purifying its water. In fact, whether it seems true in your present circumstances, you as the parent actually have the *most* control over improving your home environment.

Since none of your family members are the problem, don't add to the pollution by labeling any of them (including yourself) as such. Instead, focus your attention and energy on identifying family members' problematic thoughts or actions and how they operate in the context of your environment. As you read this book, ask questions that keep you curious about why you and your family members might think and act about technology as you and they do at any given moment. For example:

- Why did my kid's refusal to turn off the TV (or phone, or tablet, or gaming system) make me so much angrier today than it did yesterday? Is there anything else influencing how I feel right now? Like, am I really tired? Or maybe do I find that my partner reacts the same way when I suggest we turn off the TV? Or did my kid's refusal remind me that he's chronically denying my instructions?

- Why did my kid refuse to turn off the TV in the first place? What does he feel he is losing out on when he turns it off? What kinds of things could we do together that might rival the enjoyment he was having while watching TV?

- Am I uncertain about how I feel or what my kid wants because I've been preoccupied today with my own electronic device?

As you investigate your family's thoughts and actions relative to your shared environment, you will confirm that improving the environment is the solution to the problem therein. As Woody Allen observed about the environment surrounding all of us, "I hate reality, but it's the only place I can get a really good sandwich."

The Reverse Hierarchy

Whether or not you consciously thought it, what you wanted and expected when you became a parent was a chain of command that flows from parent to child. At some level of consciousness, you correctly intuited that children have three jobs:

1. School—Attending class and completing homework

2. Home—Following directions and fulfilling household responsibilities, i.e., minding parents

3. Fun–Playing

You are also correct in thinking that your primary job is to help Junior fulfill the first two, which are responsibilities, in order to access the third, which is a privilege. The reality for most children in developed countries is that fun is going to include using technology at times. You have considered this reality before and have reconciled it to some extent, perhaps deciding that fighting overuse of technology is a "good problem" to have. But even if you are completely okay with your child using technology, the overall organizational structure you have in mind looks something like this:

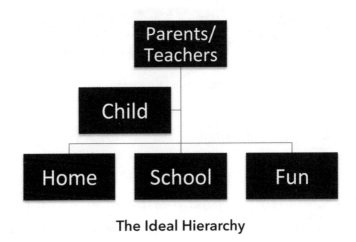

The Ideal Hierarchy

Let's refer to this diagram as the Ideal Hierarchy: the parents and teachers are united in guiding the child, who in turn balances the three jobs of being a kid.

If things have gotten pretty messy in your home with regard to screen time and determining who's in charge of it all, the chain of command has become inverted. It probably looks more like this:

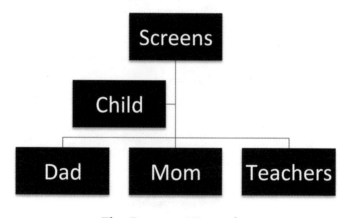

The Reverse Hierarchy

Let's refer to this diagram with a term from Family Systems called "the Reverse Hierarchy." In this scenario, technology is in charge, and the humans have become the devices. In this scenario, the sci-fi movie your kid stayed up watching last night just came true in your living room. Further, notice that the adults are the humans at the very bottom of the pecking order—and that they are fragmented.

A classic Reverse Hierarchy paradigm would be that Mom thinks Junior needs to tighten up on his responsibilities, while Dad thinks Mom is being too strict on Junior. Junior's teacher empathizes with both viewpoints but doesn't care how the parents do it, as long as they get Junior to turn in his math assignments. The difference of opinion among the adults is readily apparent to Junior, who experiences the adults as divided and conquerable. Junior determines he can sneak screen time while his parents consult their friends about how to help him get his math done. Junior has no idea how much control the game actually has of him, but he knows he is fulfilling his favorite job: fun. He knows playing the game helps compensate for the miserable time he had during math class that day. He also knows it is especially fun to thumb his nose at the fragmented system the adults cannot seem to streamline and coordinate. The game plays the kid, who plays the parents and teachers.

If you doubt whether the game is playing your kid, ask yourself why he doesn't answer when you invite him to do something as pleasurable as eat. If you doubt whether your son is playing you, ask yourself who is left frustrated at the dinner table when he keeps playing the game instead of coming to dinner. If you have had to resort to texting your son to get him to come to dinner, that's the Reverse Hierarchy captured in one interaction. The Reverse Hierarchy contributes to the pollution in your family fishbowl. But how did a Reverse Hierarchy come to reign in your home?

The Over/Under

In sports, the over/under is the predicted total number of points scored by both teams; gamblers then choose whether the actual number of points scored in the game will be higher (over) or lower (under) than that predicted. In home environments where the Reverse Hierarchy reigns, parents are working harder than kids are to solve the screen problem. So it can be said that the parent is over-functioning and the kid is under-functioning. For our purposes here, that situation is the over/under.

In the preceding Reverse Hierarchy example, when you are left frustrated at the dinner table, repeatedly calling for (or texting) your son while he's still playing the game, you're over-functioning relative to the minimal level of effort one can expect parents to put forth to invite their child to dinner. And your son is under-functioning relative to the already minimal level of effort one can expect a child to put forth to come to the table.

During a recent session in my office, some very patient parents kindly asked their teenage son how he would like them to get his attention if they needed to notify him of dinnertime while he was wearing a headset and playing a video game. They told me they'd tried calling to their son, but he did not seem to hear them. They asked their son if they should knock on his door instead. He replied with the following imperative: "Come tap on my headset, and I will talk to you."

His parents were just about to agree to do so when I stopped them. I pointed out that in such a scenario, the game would have come to command such power that the boy couldn't even respond to his parents (even when they were calling him for dinner!). I suggested that the game was essentially playing the parents as well, making them tantamount to butlers by requiring them to travel to their son's room, walk to him, and tap on his headset so that he would grant them a moment before his throne of entertainment.

Had it played out, the preceding scenario would have constituted another classic Reverse Hierarchy, with Junior under-functioning and Mom and Dad over-functioning. It's no fun to discover the Reverse Hierarchy and the over/under are operating within your home. So let me remind you that we're taking the time to do so because placing your family's screen problem in context is necessary preparation for improving that context.

Red Herrings

In addition to the over/under and the ways it gives rise to the Reverse Hierarchy, parents' misdirected questions about technology sometimes cause or perpetuate problems in the home environment. Misdirected questions that cannot be answered or lead to erroneous conclusions are called red herrings—no fishbowl pun intended!

In my practice, I have seen parents futilely chase four red herrings in particular. I will phrase each of these red herrings as a question, address it, and pose new questions that are more answerable and informative.

Red Herring #1: The opening pages of this chapter refer to the "electronics addiction." Is it really an addiction, per se?

The simple answer is that while the amount of dopamine released in the brain is high, your child is not. He does not enter an altered state of consciousness by gaming, and he will not become "addicted" in the same way he would get hooked on a drug. So don't worry about (or get caught up in debating your partner about) whether to call it an addiction. Instead, focus on the simple fact that a functional dependence on gaming—whether you label it an addiction for short—is a problem worth solving. To determine whether your child is (or is becoming) functionally dependent on screens, look for warning signs that he is being played, rather than doing the playing.

Ask yourself:

- Do all of my child's discussions ultimately lead to the game?

- Does his tech dependence negatively impact his school performance?

- Does gaming or tech use get in the way of other activities and commitments like playing with friends, performing household tasks and chores, participating in extracurricular activities, or accompanying me on an errand?

You've asked yourself many of these questions already, which is why you picked up this book. Even if you answer yes to each one, your solution will not be to hold an intervention or otherwise treat your child like an addict. Instead, remember the temptation of the forbidden fruity power button. Your child's desire for technology is understandable and age appropriate. Thinking about your child's desire in such ways will help you stay calm enough to implement the solution to his screen problem. Remember, that's the problem we're fixing and it's communal. We're not fixing your kid.

Red Herring #2: Is the problem inside my child's brain?

Your child might seek copious amounts of screen time to boost a deficient level of dopamine, so one might argue that the problem is a chemical imbalance that exists inside your child's brain. But this would be a psychiatric definition of the problem, implicating neurotransmitters and neurochemicals and calling for help through medication.

As a psychologist, I wrote this book to help families think, feel, and act in ways that promote health for each member and for the group as a unit. So merely placing the problem "inside your child's brain" would be a red herring, because you will find that the solution proposed in this book is effective whether or not your child is medicated for a neurochemical imbalance. Instead of limiting the location of the problem to your child's brain, get curious about how your child thinks, feels, and acts as a result of what's going on in and around her. This includes not only what's happening inside her brain, but also what's happening inside her body and within her family, her peer group, her school, and even the interplay among these entities. For example, you might ask yourself:

- How might I make sense of how whimsically my daughter changes her status on social-media websites? Is there something she finds empowering about doing so?

- If so, might this act of exercising control over her self-expression make sense, given what she's told me about how stressful she finds her school day or how powerless she seems to feel in some social situations?

- How might she be using an online conversation as a means of getting perspective on a disappointing grade or a troubling social interaction?

Red Herring #3: Is gaming inherently bad for the brain? Does it negatively impact intelligence? And since smartphones have games, are they bad for the developing brain too?

Wouldn't that be nice and clear—if gaming were as obviously bad for your child as something like cigarettes? But it is not. Certainly, gaming and technology *can* be unhealthy, but it depends on how they're used.

Concerns about gaming being damaging to the brain are more red herrings. Your child already knows this and has evidence to challenge such a position if you argue it. The evidence your child has amassed might include a recent international study documenting, within gamers, increased brain volume in areas that manage important functions like memory and planning (Kuhn and colleagues, 2013) or a recent *American Psychologist* meta-analysis that reviewed studies documenting various cognitive and emotional benefits of gaming (Granic, Lobel, and Engels, 2014). Cognitive benefits include enhanced memory, perception, navigation, creativity, reasoning, and problem solving, while emotional benefits include improved mood, increased relaxation and emotional resilience, decreased anxiety, and the establishment of virtual social communities.

You will rightly lose the argument if you try to appeal to the "fact" that kids simply "shouldn't be gaming because it's bad for them." The game is not the problem, but it might be being used in a problematic fashion that carries negative ramifications for your child's brain or development. So consider how the game or electronic device is impacting your child's performance at school and his behavior at home, and ask yourself the following questions:

- Is Junior playing games that are rated for older audiences?

- Is he using his phone to access inappropriate content?

- Does he lose sleep while doing so?

- Have I caught him lying about what he plays or views?

Pursuing answers to questions like these will help you determine if the game or device has come to constitute a threat to your child's brain or development.

Red Herring #4: Is society to blame for my family's screen problem?

Some parents might argue that the real problem is "society" or "culture" or "the media." This is a legitimate position; perhaps the genesis of the problem is one of these macro factors. But this, too, is a red herring, because your ability to mediate the role of such entities in your home is the most important factor of all. While the content that finds its way through technology into your home might sometimes trouble you, you can decide how to respond to it by deciding whether to turn any given device on in the first place, and by determining in any given moment whether the content it's transmitting is beneficial, threatening, or neutral.

Again, it all depends on context. How to categorize a game or device on any given day depends on what it's transmitting and how it's being used. Obviously, don't treat technology as inherently good and make it king of your home. Equally as dangerous, but less obvious, don't treat technology as benign and let it creep to the top of a Reverse Hierarchy in your home. Last, don't write off technology as inherently evil and necessary to avoid—at some point you might need it, and you'll almost certainly want it. Instead of making any of these mistakes, categorize each electronic device for what it is: a convenience whose contribution to your environment is constantly being determined— not by your child, and certainly not by the apparatus itself, but by *you*. Ask yourself:

- Is my family treating our tech as benign, without really thinking this through?

- What's the nature or content of what we're viewing?

- Are we neglecting important responsibilities in favor of gaming?

- Are we revering our devices as "safe havens" that we all seek at the end of the day?

- Do we spend time in the same room but in front of our personal devices and claim that we're having "family time"?

Trust Your Gut

Especially after finding out that some of the questions they had are red herrings, most parents I consult with aren't sure how reliable their instincts about technology and managing screen time are. In case you're one of them, here are the five instincts that you need to know are correct so that you can trust them implicitly. Getting your fishbowl clean hinges upon your following these instincts, so I will orient you to them throughout the book. I encourage you to memorize them or, better yet, to look within yourself and follow them over and over, noticing how reliably they guide you.

Instinct #1: Technology Stimulates

Jerry Seinfeld recalls his bedtime routine from childhood as follows: "My bedtime story when I was a kid? Darkness!" Contrast this experience with that of my adolescent client who recently told me that he determines his bedtime this way: "When there are no YouTube videos left to watch, I go to sleep."

Does my client's way of determining his bedtime sit well with you? If not, then your Technology Stimulates instinct is intact. By and large, technology for kids is an upper, not a downer—it tends to have more of a stimulating than a calming effect.

The enjoyment of technology increases the flow of dopamine, and the excitement of the game boosts adrenaline, while the blue light emitted by the screen inhibits the production of melatonin, a natural sleep agent. As such, UCLA psychiatrist Dr. Peter Whybrow aptly refers to computers as "electronic cocaine" (Thompson, 2014).

Certainly, many adults fall asleep to the TV or nod off while reading an e-book (though hopefully not this one), and children might do the same on occasion. But if you're having the feeling that maybe Junior would be better rested and behaved if he took a little screen hiatus, then trust your gut: you're probably right. If you sense that maybe he would fall asleep more easily if he wasn't wondering whether a text was about to vibrate the phone hidden under his pillow, then trust your gut: you're *definitely* right.

That second one seems like a self-evident truth, doesn't it? Yet as adults, we struggle ourselves with powering down and getting enough sleep. I recently heard about an adult who went to complete a sleep study at a clinic to determine why he was suffering from insomnia. As part of the study, he was required to turn over all electronic devices. He promptly slept for fourteen straight hours! Upon awakening and learning how long he had slept, he was struck by the fact that his insomnia mustn't have been some mysterious problem inside his brain. Instead, he observed to one of the staff that perhaps knowing that there would be no opportunity to log on to or be contacted by way of an electronic device all night was all that was necessary for him to sleep soundly. The staff member replied, "Yep! It happens here all the time."

Instinct #2: Dodge Friendly Fire

As a necessary part of growing up, your child is going to make shortsighted choices from time to time, and you cannot prevent all of them (without becoming overprotective and stifling her maturation). Your gut is accurate when it tells you that truly learning something sometimes requires experiencing it. The parents of a three-year-old girl can turn off and put away the tablet when it's bedtime. But when the same girl turns ten years old, her parents will not be able to (nor should they) prevent the sleepover when she and her friends first conquer staying up all night by enjoying a movie marathon and inadvertently render themselves irritable and lethargic for a day.

When your child makes shortsighted choices you can't or shouldn't prevent, you must shift from prevention mode to damage-control mode. However, the damage control is not about repairing things for your child, it's about what you might call "ducking and covering." During war, you protect yourself from enemy attack while also dodging friendly fire when necessary. You don't step in front of your troops to lecture them while they're trying to shoot. If your daughter is moody after a sleepover, you both need space more immediately than she needs a talking-to. Space will preserve your day, while that talking-to might ruin both of your days.

Recall the over/under: You can't care more about the outcome of her choice (like her mood after staying up all night) than she does. So give yourself permission simply to do what you can to facilitate sound decision making (as will be detailed in chapter 3) and then to protect yourself from the collateral damage caused by shortsighted choices.

Instinct #3: Two Marshmallows Are Better Than One

If you intuited that being successful depends in part on being able to delay gratification, you were right. And the importance of being able to wait is evident early on: kids who can stay patient and wait to be rewarded with a bigger prize tend to outperform kids who can't wait and instead settle for an immediate, but smaller, prize.

In 1970 psychologist Walter Mischel arranged an experiment at Stanford University wherein preschoolers were invited to make a difficult decision. Would they opt for one marshmallow now or two marshmallows several minutes later? More than ten years later, the researchers followed up with the participants. Those who had been able to inhibit the impulse to take one marshmallow now in favor of two later were enjoying significantly more optimal functioning in adolescence, as measured by variables like performance on the Scholastic Aptitude Test (SAT), school grades, and body mass index (BMI).

The kids who waited had established something psychologists call "object permanence," the understanding that things not immediately accessible in plain sight can still exist or have existed and can often even be obtained later. Permanent objects can be real things, like the second marshmallow, or intangible experiences, like feeling happy. Trusting in the existence and value of permanent objects lends itself to willpower and self-control during the unforgiving moments when mere observation might otherwise suggest such objects aren't real, don't matter, or aren't worth waiting for. For Junior to trust you that he'll obtain something better later by being able to turn off the TV now, you'll need to help him establish object permanence so he can wait for that proverbial second marshmallow.

Instinct #4: Actions Speak

Behavior communicates even when words don't. Poker champions describe making good moves by being able to read their opponents' nonverbal tells, not by listening to what their opponents say.

You know the feeling you get when you think Junior might be bluffing. You know the degree of privilege you should grant him hinges more on how he acts than on what he says during his verbal appeal. You are wise to encourage him to demonstrate for you through his behavior (rather than overpromise to you through his words) the degree of privilege he can handle at present. If he presents cogent arguments for attending a late-night gaming session at a friend's house, but he's already tired, hasn't finished his book report, and has been grumpy all day, you can expect him to come home even grumpier, more fatigued, and in no condition to finish the report, despite his promises to the contrary. If he presents the same arguments after having been energized, pleasant, and productive all day, then maybe he can handle the gaming session and will come back to you no worse for the wear.

Instinct #5: Garbage In, Garbage Out

In studies that rely on statistics, findings are only as valid as the data they are based on. If you put crummy data into a statistical formula, that's exactly what you get out. So too, your gut is telling you the truth when it senses that what your child watches or engages in will impact how he speaks, thinks, and acts. Remember, the fish takes in the water and puts it back out.

A 2013 study published in *Educational Media International* suggests that playing more than three hours a day of violent video games correlates with interference in the development of sentiments like empathy and skills like ethical reasoning. A great mentor of mine suggested that carrying such sentiments and skills depended on the calibration of a capacity he called "the moral compass." The moral compass is an anchored sense of self and purpose that directs us in our lives and relationships.

I recently spoke with a local father who is involved in various community organizations. He had attended a parenting workshop where he said the audience was encouraged to buy their sons an old-school pornographic magazine in order to provide a relatively less crude set of stimuli than the boys were likely stumbling onto online. Perhaps the speaker at the workshop had heard the same observation that I have heard parents make: "Putting your kid in his room with unmitigated Internet access and asking him to stay off porn sites is like putting him in his room with a stack of *Playboys* and asking him not to open any of them."

So while the suggestion to provide one porno mag instead of unmitigated Internet access to all kinds of porn sounds well intentioned to me, the suggestion also reminds me of advertisements for "leaner, healthier" fast food that's nonetheless processed. The bottom line is that the suggestion still entails handing porn to kids. That idea just doesn't sit quite right with you, does it? Does that sound like the way to calibrate the moral compass? I heard a troubling stat the other day: eleven years is the average age at which kids first encounter pornography. Ugh. Fellow parents, we can do better.

When I spoke with that local father, he told me that his gut also sensed that something about the suggestion was amiss. He was tuning in to his Garbage In, Garbage Out instinct. We talked about how old-school porno magazines and contemporary online porn videos share some of the same drawbacks: objectification of women (and men), unrealistic representations of sexual encounters and aftermaths, an illusion of intimacy between the viewer and the model or actors, and so forth. The father decided that in either case—magazines or the Internet—his son ingesting pornography was not going to foster the kind of relationships he hoped for him to have with girls as he progressed through his adolescence, or with women as he entered adulthood. The father recognized that old-school porno mags pollute the water just like online videos do. He decided not to buy his son the magazine and to continue monitoring his online activity.

Whoa! The thought of kids encountering porn at eleven years old, the prospect of helping our children enjoy future romantic relationships, myriad questions about their brain development, dreams of improving their grades, longings for healthy family functioning in our homes . . . The stakes of this game we're playing together couldn't be higher. Let's get a clearer sense of all that's on the line by determining just how big the problem is.

Chapter 2

The Scope of the Problem

"Whoops! I shouldn't have sent that!"
—All of us, at one point or another

As defined in chapter 1, macro factors are overarching phenomena that impact life inside each fishbowl. One such phenomenon currently under debate in our world is Internet privacy. Can a balance be struck between monitoring electronic communications in the name of safety and *not* monitoring electronic communications in the name of privacy?

Even if you have strong opinions on the international events surrounding this question, you may find yourself less clear about what to do within your home. You know it's important to grant your kids privacy, but you're trying to balance that privacy with ensuring they are safe and engaging appropriately with others. So imbalance is part of your family's screen problem. Where's the line? How is balance achieved?

Your Family's Department of Health and Safety

Let's work backward, starting with what's already clear: it's dangerous to "default" to either over- or under-monitoring your child's activity. Follow your Dodge Friendly Fire instinct: The danger of over-monitoring is that you're over-functioning. You stifle your child's growth and engender resentment because your child feels like she doesn't have her space. While your child never makes a mistake, she never really learns for herself, either. She learns to under-function while you prevent her from making mistakes or absorb all the consequences of her mistakes. There's no learning by experience.

The danger of under-monitoring is that one of your greatest fears comes true: your daughter ends up sending naked selfies to someone she thinks is a handsome peer a few states away, when the anonymous online partner is actually your adult neighbor. (Not that sending naked selfies to a handsome peer is safe or appropriate either.)

The dangers of over- and under-monitoring are clear. But deciding how to provide an appropriate level of monitoring is really tough because there are no cookie-cutter approaches that will work every time. You'll have to take it case by case, but use the following analogy as a rule of thumb to help you decide on the level of monitoring a given situation requires.

Imagine that you work as the director of your family's very own Department of Health and Safety. Your dual role in the department is to promote health, which includes upholding your child's privacy as long as she is conducting herself appropriately, and to ensure safety at all costs. If upholding her privacy means she can conduct herself inappropriately or behave unsafely, then privacy temporarily might have to take second place because appropriate conduct and safe behavior take precedence over her feeling comfortable or happy with you.

The Health and Safety philosophy is essentially the basis for the limits of confidentiality that exist between psychologists and adult clients. Psychologists' ethical code requires us to keep information private until an identified person's safety is at risk. At that point, the psychologist has to work to promote safety, even if doing so violates privacy.

So determining the answers to questions like . . .

- Should I read my child's texts?
- Should I search her room for electronics that are off limits?
- Is she ready for her own social-media account?
- Do I need to review what she posts on Instagram?

. . . depends heavily on your observations of how appropriate your child's conduct is and how safe her behaviors are. Tap into your Garbage In, Garbage Out instinct and ask yourself what your child is being exposed to, and also access your Actions Speak instinct and ask yourself what your child's actions say.

- Is your child evidencing that she is unsafe to herself or others?
- Is she cutting herself, even superficially, with any sharp object?
- Does she make verbal threats to peers or family members when she's upset?
- Does she engage in high-risk behaviors like drinking alcohol or using drugs?
- When her friends come over, do they talk with her about dangerous subject matter?

- Have her friends quit coming over, and she's also quit telling you where she's going when she leaves to hang out with them?

- Would she avoid telling you or another trustworthy adult if one of her friends disclosed to her that they were in danger?

- Has she exhibited a sudden and unexpected shift in behavior?

- Do her friends' parents report that their kids are engaging in sexting and other lewd behaviors?

- Does she slam the top of the laptop the minute you walk in the room?

- Do you catch her lying about matters of safety?

If you answered yes to any of these questions, then you need to (continue to) decisively monitor your child's activities to help ensure that her conduct is appropriate and that she is behaving safely. Her activities include those that are technological in nature, like texting, gaming, posting online, viewing online content, and the like. So yes, you probably need to monitor those activities even if she doesn't like it. Do so until you have no evidence that she's using the electronics at hand in ways that expose her to inappropriate or unsafe practices or that allow her to engage in such practices herself.

As you're determining how much privacy to grant your child with regard to electronics use, remember that you can gather information in a variety of ways: gently asking questions, listening without pressure to share or judgment about what she does share, modeling how to share thoughts and feelings in the first place, spending quality downtime together, encouraging your child to regularly invite her friends over, and so forth.

The more of these questions you can answer affirmatively, the more private electronics use you can safely grant:

- Do your child's actions reflect that her mood is relatively stable and that she is generally content?

- Can she avoid verbally attacking her peers and family members even when she's upset with them?

- Is she home at curfew after reliably going where she said she'd be?

- When you walk in her room, does she typically let you take a glance at what she's viewing on her screen or at least not try to hide it?

- Does she tell you about her struggles and ask for your help?

- Do you have *zero* evidence that she's at risk of harming herself or anyone else or that any of her acquaintances are in any kind of danger?

If you answered yes to all these questions, then perhaps you have no ostensible cause for concern about the riskiness of your child's electronic or nonelectronic activities. Great! Stay cautiously optimistic, keep your degree of monitoring relatively low, and seize the opportunity to thereby demonstrate to your child that you respect her privacy.

If you can't get the information you need to feel solid about how much privacy to grant your child with regard to electronics use, then you might not be able to grant much privacy. Err on the side of caution in terms of monitoring, because as your child develops, the importance of safe behavior and appropriate conduct trumps the importance of privacy.

An Intimate Evening with the Entire World

What about the other way around? What if your kid is way too inclusive with her disclosures, telling people more private information than appropriate, causing a safety issue of a different sort? What should you do if she's not keeping secrets from you but she's not maintaining her own privacy either?

To answer these questions, you might first ask yourself: "If I were to have a birthday party and feel really celebrated, whom would I invite over to hang out in my backyard?" If you're quite sociable, your answer might be, "A ton of friends—the whole office!" But your answer wouldn't be "The whole world!" because you know how risky that would be.

Without your help protecting her privacy, your child is inviting the entire world into her bedroom by way of electronic devices. It's ironic that the name of the original monolith social network, MySpace, could be considered a misnomer. Would a more apt name for the network have been Everyone'sSpace? How well would that name have gone over with your savvy kid?

The essential point to help your child grasp is that social-networking sites are not electronic diaries, virtual landfills where we can safely dump emotional garbage that will eventually decompose. They're just the opposite: places where virtual garbage exists in perpetuity. You want to help your child learn how to prevent that feeling you've had after you send an e-mail and then realize, "Oh, man. I really shouldn't have sent that."

You can expect your child to respond to your point with something along these lines: "Mom, come on—I can set my privacy settings really high. I don't rant and rave about sensitive topics on Facebook, and only a few of my friends can read what I post anyway. And I trust *all* of them."

On one hand, that's great! Your child might be using the networking site appropriately. On the other hand, she might be extending trust to someone she shouldn't. Consider the examples you've heard about sexual partners trusting one another enough to make a sex tape, only to have one partner later publicize the tape. What's more, your child might indeed be engaging with trustworthy peers while inadvertently putting plenty of data out there for the hungry hacker or wily predator. Indeed, there are ways that others can unlock protected electronic content. Electronic content is really only protected to an extent.

Remember, you're the director of your family's Department of Health and Safety. What do you observe?

- Is your child trading posts with some unidentified adult who could be a predator living around the corner?

- Is your teen's status on her social-media account an acronym you aren't familiar with, such as *DTF*? When you look up the acronym, does its meaning suggest your daughter is available for indiscriminate sexual activity?

- Is your younger child playing first-person shooter (FPS) games on "teams" made up of total strangers, who your child admits "swear at each other a lot" but insists "are really nice guys" and "they even want to hang out in person sometime"?

Answering yes to any of these questions suggests a safety risk. Chapters 5 through 7 will highlight specific courses of action you can take to help ensure safety, but the bottom line here is that your degree of monitoring must be high and your child's degree of private tech use must be low.

Virtual Insanity

A few months ago, I spoke at a parent-teacher association meeting, and a mother shared that her teenage son nearly suffered a panic attack when she asked him to call a local pizzeria to place a delivery order. He complained that he didn't have any experience calling anyone, especially a business, and that he was only adept at texting. The mother described how she had to model the behavior for her son and train him to be able to *call* for pizza.

More recently in my office, a mother noted her concern that her teenage daughter never answers her cell phone, but rather replies later to her mother's voice mails by sending a text. And the father of one of my adolescent clients observed just the other day, "[Electronics] is the world he's comfortable in." What is going on in these scenarios? Let's look to a classic video game for an apt analogy that might help us answer this question.

At the end of each "world" or level in the original Super Mario Bros. Nintendo game, Mario runs the gauntlet of a new castle and defeats its overlord in an effort to rescue the princess—but he invariably learns the real princess is actually being detained in a different castle. The same scenario manifests in real life for the isolated gamer. His future partner, if he's ever going to find one, is far away . . . in another castle. But he isn't socially connected enough to know to be disappointed.

He's socially comfortable only at a distance, so all he knows is to keep on playing. He doesn't grasp that his virtual accomplishments aren't real, that he hasn't truly come in "contact" with anyone by way of the game. There's no real relationship there. Virtual socialization might be healthy to an extent, but it's not sufficient. It's pseudo-engagement, pseudo-intimacy. That's why, after two adults become intrigued by one another through an online dating service, they typically want to get together in person.

I do not mean to suggest that you should be worried about introducing Junior to his future partner before he graduates kindergarten. The idea is that real relationships, from friendships to romantic partnerships, occur between two people in a context of real time and physical proximity. This idea sounds obvious, yet so many of us settle for connecting virtually. We decide to forego the road trip to visit Grandma, and just FaceTime her instead. We go to a party but spend a fair amount of time checking updates on our smartphones instead of socializing with the people there. And some of us even decide not to meet the real person behind the intriguing dating profile.

Why? We probably settle for connecting virtually because doing so feels at the time like anything but settling. Connecting virtually is often more comfortable and is sometimes more stimulating than connecting with someone in reality. Connecting virtually by texting, for example, can eliminate awkward silences, buy you time to think before you reply, and allow you to participate in multiple conversations or information streams at once. You can carry on a couple of text conversations while also checking Twitter and your news app and taking your turn in a game of Words with Friends. But the reality is that you are only able to participate in elements of each of these activities at any given time. You're actually checking out of the present moment, not tuning in to it. By definition, it's impossible to focus your full attention on multiple things simultaneously. And you neglect whatever or whoever is right in front of your face . . . er . . . in front of your face but behind your phone.

Take, on the other hand, the prospect of connecting with someone in reality, and let's say neither of you has an electronic device to retreat into. Some readers will recall the awkward moments they spent as teens when they went on first dates and there were no cell phones to carry into the restaurant for "backup," and there were few screens on the walls of the establishment that could supply conversation fodder. Those dates were tough, but we made it through them. In fact, what a gift it is to have had them! Talk about a good problem. Those awkward moments were the ones where authentic, organic connections could be made because part of participating in those types of moments together is experiencing the silence in all of its awkwardness . . . developing the patience to roll with social and emotional exchanges that ebb and flow in their level of stimulation or intensity . . . really tuning in with the person across from you . . . getting creative about where to go next in the dialogue.

So you can anticipate that your child will sometimes accuse you of offering less stimulating alternatives to staying glued to the screen. Good! You're doing your child a favor by offering real, longer-lasting, although sometimes less intensely stimulating experiences. Your job isn't to constantly supply equally appealing alternatives to electronics, though offering suggestions of some such options will certainly help your child make the better choice at times. Imagine the ultimate result if you were constantly able to offer really comfortable yet stimulating alternatives to electronics use. Your kid would become dependent on a steady diet of unchallenging but entertaining stimuli—a dependency that would take him even further out of real relationships than you currently find him to be. Now *that* would certainly be an electronics addiction.

Yes, reality bites sometimes. But remember the Woody Allen quote: reality is where you find the good sandwich. The sandwich is good *precisely because* it's real, not because it's exciting or comfortable.

Now that you've read the first two chapters, you have become the expert on your family's screen problem. You have situated the problem in a context that takes account of the interactions among family members and of larger societal influences. You have determined that the scope of the problem is very broad. So what can we do about it? What can we do to make the digital age the era of truly reconnecting with others instead of just plugging into our devices? What we realistically can do and also what we need to do starts within our homes and spreads from there, like a computer virus but without the destruction. What we're going to implement in our homes is a novel solution to the problem of your polluted fishbowl. Let us pass the solution along to others like we're making it go viral. The object of Step II is to embrace this solution. Doing so begins with understanding how our kids learn so that we can teach them healthier and more fulfilling ways of navigating the world.

STEP II:

Embrace a Novel Solution

Chapter 3

How Kids Learn

"Tell me and I forget, teach me and I may remember, involve me and I learn."
—Benjamin Franklin

There are three primary pathways through which kids learn:
1) Instruction—What they are told
2) Observation—What they see modeled for them
3) Outcomes—What they experience as a result of their behavior

Consider the learning process that occurs when a novice snowboarder takes a lesson from an Olympic snowboard champion. The novice listens to the pro, who offers *instruction*, telling the novice how deeply to bend her knees or where to aim the board. The novice also *observes* the pro as she models the act of confidently snowboarding down the mountain and off the jump. The novice's mirror neurons fire and thereby begin to wire the novice's brain to perform the action herself. The novice then attempts a run by herself, promptly face-plants, and uses this most undesirable *outcome* as information to guide her subsequent attempts, or perhaps to guide her to a decision to give up on snowboarding altogether!

Based on the quote in the chapter epigraph, Benjamin Franklin would likely say that *involvement* occurs when the three pathways align. It's pretty difficult to enforce limits on screen time if you can talk the talk but can't walk the walk. It is unlikely that Junior is going to follow your instruction to turn off his video game and instead complete his assigned reading if you are commanding him to do so while anchored to your throne in front of your own computer. Junior's observation of you passing countless hours in front of your screen silently implies that it is your most prized possession. He understandably questions if perhaps he will find his time best spent in front of a screen as well.

This kind of modeling also implies that you are a hypocrite because you cannot follow your own advice and turn off your screen. Demonstrating hypocrisy does little to engender trust and connection. If you want Junior to listen to you about much of anything, you have to demonstrate integrity by having your instruction match how he observes you living. When instruction and observation differ, Junior is going to follow the path of lesser resistance. Smart kid! Considering the context, he's making a perfectly understandable and reasonable choice. He has come to learn that using the screen is the easier choice—and the one you make for yourself.

When it comes to kids and tech use, how you help your child navigate these first two learning pathways is critical, because the third path, outcomes, might as well be a Minecraft shaft coated with a slippery layer of pure dopamine. Think about it: Junior's tech use is an exhilarating experience whose dopamine release represents a much more pleasurable outcome than what he experiences while chipping away at his assigned reading.

Homework is already no match for electronics use, so don't exacerbate the mismatch in outcomes by offering modeling (or instruction) that would further encourage him to choose screens over homework. The mismatch is apparent when Junior veers away from a screen-based homework assignment and onto his favorite Internet sites. To help you align the three paths so you know what to do in situations involving this mismatch and others that are similar, let's examine each path a bit more closely.

Instruction

Instruction is pretty obvious but not completely. If you want your child to do one thing, you wouldn't verbally tell him to do its opposite. What about when your partner has told your child one thing and you notice yourself stating its opposite?

This scenario does not mean that either you or your partner must be wrong—but it does highlight fragmentation between the adults, which you will recall from chapter 1 is one problematic component of the Reverse Hierarchy. Privately get on the same page with your partner. There are many parenting books that address this process, so I will not go into detail here. All you need to know for now is the answer to this question: If one parent says it's time for homework and the other says it's time for play, which parent is your child going to listen to?

Observation

Especially during adolescence, your child is going to look more at what you do than listen to what you say. What you model for anyone who looks up to you, especially your child, will necessarily impact how she acts. Recall from your college Psych 101 course the famous Bobo doll experiment of the early 1960s, led by psychologist Albert Bandura. During this landmark study, preschoolers watched a boy beat up on an inflatable plastic toy called Bobo, whose weighted base allowed him to pop back up after being knocked down. After watching the boy beat up the doll, the preschoolers—without any verbal instruction to do so—began acting more aggressively with one another.

Think also of your last girls' night out or golf day with the guys. You might have heard choice words slipping out of your own mouth more than usual, just because you were hearing them uttered around you. What might have been the drink talking was also the Bobo effect in action.

The reason for this effect is that what we observe can quickly and easily influence how we act. It's that simple. You already sensed this truth via your Garbage In, Garbage Out instinct. This fact is the rationale for employing discretion when determining how graphic a movie or video game to allow your child to watch or play. Employing discretion requires the act of asking a very simple question—let's call it the Bobo Question: "Do

I want my child acting like what he's wanting to watch or play?"

I recently saw a boy in my office who had been acting aggressively at school. Consistent with my use of the Family Systems framework, his parents were also present for the session. The boy was trying to convince his parents that he wasn't acting aggressively at school as a function of playing violent video games. A former office mate once gifted me a T-shirt that read, "I'm all over that like Bandura on Bobo." I might as well have been wearing that shirt during this session—I had already asked the parents the Bobo Question and encouraged them to follow their Actions Speak and Garbage In, Garbage Out instincts, so the boy's argument fell flat. The adults knew that the boy couldn't help but be influenced, at least to some degree, by the video games he was playing. How he was acting within the games of course influenced to some extent how he was acting at school.

Following our instincts and answering the Bobo Question made setting a goal very straightforward: The boy needed to maintain appropriate conduct at school, thereby demonstrating he was ready for his parents to gradually reintroduce some of the games he preferred. If he could manage his real-world conduct even after playing the video games, then he would be allowed to continue playing them.

It takes a considerable degree of self-control to engage in a violent game or become enthralled in a really intense movie and then immediately to act appropriately with the real people in your life once you turn the screen off. Don't place that burden on your child until he can really handle it. Even some of us adults can't always healthfully handle the gap we create when we toggle between reality and fantasy. So that might mean we choose not to watch certain shows, such as sensational news programs. Here, what's good for the gander is good for the goose; our kids are watching us to see what we watch.

Our kids are watching us to see what we watch in terms of its content, and they're also watching us to see what we're not paying attention to instead, like:

- Their soccer game. Are we following them or something on our tablets?

- Mealtimes. Are we looking at our family's faces, or are we only "together" with them inasmuch as we are watching scripted family interactions on TV?

- Family meetings. While discussing important family decisions, are we reading our family members' body language or our texts?

- Driving. Are we looking where we're going in order to model and ensure safety, or are we watching the smartphone's progress as it downloads an e-mail?

- Their nonelectronic playtime. Are we admiring our children as they build a Lego spaceship, or are we admiring our own progress at a specific game app?

Yes, I know one is more comfortable and perhaps more stimulating. But which one's more magnificent?

If you need to do so in order to model healthy habits or to prevent your tech from playing you, schedule half-hour blocks of the day (ideally when your child is at school or in bed) when you'll wholly attend to your screen-based activities and complete your tech-based responsibilities. Do this instead of letting your tech repeatedly pull you out of the present moment, especially if that moment is one you're sharing with your kid.

Mahatma Gandhi urged followers to "be the change you wish to see in the world." If we have any hope of changing our families, let alone the world, we must "be" relative to our electronic devices the ways we wish for others to be as well.

Outcomes

Let's say that your instruction matches what your child observes you to be modeling: You aren't on your computer all day and you turn it off when it's time to wind down before bedtime, which you do by reading. The computer doesn't own you. And let's say your son isn't watching inappropriate stuff online and his conduct is good. Yet when you ask him to turn off his computer and complete his school reading before bed, he's still choosing against you.

Why? He's still choosing against you because the outcomes of his choice to play (dopamine, adrenaline, pleasure, thrill) are still more appealing than the outcomes of the choice to read (semi-entertainment, mostly critical thinking, appeasing you, chance at a better grade). He's choosing privilege—the job of having fun—over responsibility, the jobs of minding you and doing his schoolwork. His behavior makes sense. There's no reason to fix your kid. Rather, you will need to temporarily modify the environment so that the outcomes of reading rival the outcomes of playing, both by rewarding reading and implementing a cost associated with continuing to play (such as losing out on the next day's screen time). We're about to go into how to do this in great detail, but the general idea is to help the outcomes path run parallel with the paths of instruction and modeling.

Outcomes is a term from behaviorism, a school of psychological thought that precedes our friend Bobo. Behaviorism basically says that the outcome of our last behavior helps predict our next behavior. We learn, in part, by experience, as your Dodge Friendly Fire instinct will tell you. Recall the novice snowboarder's response to her inaugural face-plant: she makes one or more modifications to avoid the initial painful outcome and seize a more pleasant one, like staying upright on the snowboard, choosing skiing instead if she finds it easier, or even just going back to the lodge to warm up.

As an educated parent, you will not be surprised that being rewarded or punished after one behavior tends to influence the next behavior. But what might surprise you is that, in addition to basic reward and punishment, there exist two other kinds of outcomes.

The Tree

The Tree is a pictorial framework we will use several times throughout this book. The Tree depicts the ways behaviors result in outcomes.

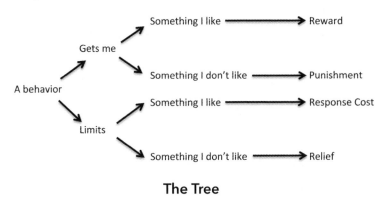

The Tree

Reading across the Tree: A given behavior either gets you something or limits something. You either like or dislike the thing being gotten or limited and thereby experience one of four outcomes, accordingly. The top scenario, or branch, serves as a reminder that when your behavior gets you something you like, by definition, you experience reward. You eat and enjoy the taste of the food and the feeling of satiety. The second branch suggests that when your behavior gets you something you don't like, you encounter a basic form of punishment. You upset your partner and get yelled at.

Reading across the third branch: When your behavior limits something you like, you encounter a variant of basic punishment called response cost. You speed and you get (and pay) a ticket. And the bottom branch reflects that when your behavior limits something you don't like, you experience relief. You take ibuprofen to alleviate a headache.

Let's look at each branch more closely and see how they hold up over time. You'll want to lean primarily on the two stronger branches.

Reward

Rewards are powerful in shaping behavior simply because people (and other animals), want what we want. We seek pleasure, as Sigmund Freud explained, via the pleasure principle. Of the four outcomes depicted in the Tree, reward is the most effective in shaping long-term behavior. You could say that the branch leading to reward constitutes the strongest branch of the Tree. So in embracing our solution to your family's screen problem, we'll lean on the reward branch the most.

Rewards are so powerful that they can have their desired impact independent of instruction and observation. For example, you can train a chicken to dance, or even play tic-tac-toe, simply by rewarding each target movement with a food pellet. You don't have to instruct the chicken or demonstrate the target movement for the chicken to learn it. Initially, you have to supply the pellet immediately enough that the chicken associates it with the behavior it just performed. If the chicken doesn't make the association, then learning (that it made the correct move) can't occur.

Over time, you can supply fewer pellets and with longer delays—even waiting as the chicken performs the whole series of moves because doing so has become habitual and consistently gets the chicken what it wants. Junior is much smarter than a chicken; you can instruct him and model for him, and he's motivated by more things than just food, so shaping his behavior might as well be even easier.

After you and Junior identify agreed-upon rewards (and we are about to cover how to do so), be sure to help him connect his undertaking the desired behavior with the reward by immediately reinforcing him with a slot-machine-like pellet that marks his progress. For example, even if it's not feasible for Junior to hit the jackpot and play a video game instantaneously after he takes out the trash, you can alert him to the fact that you're tallying his screen time the very moment he begins the act of taking out the trash. Then, continue alerting him to the fact that you are tallying as he completes the task.

There are multiple ways to alert him to the fact that you're tallying his earnings. For example, you can do so verbally. Keep it simple. Try something like: "Thanks, bud! That's worth two minutes of screen time right there" as he hauls the trash out of the house and then, "Great! There's another two minutes" when he comes back in after completing the chore. Over time, you'll be able to supply fewer pellets of reinforcement across the course of the behavior.

Another way to alert him to your tallying would be to use a baseball pitch counter and click one point or one minute of screen time for every step he takes toward completing the desired behavior. Yet another option would be to use an app to track your child's tallies. Whichever method(s) you choose, you'll also want to display the cumulative tally somewhere Junior can see it and track his progress. As he sees his tallies accumulate, he'll trust that you indeed have been documenting his earnings.

If you have older kids, you'll probably most often use a verbal notification that a reward has been earned and you probably won't need a chart showing the cumulative tally. Let's say your teen daughter earns a new app by making curfew. You can briefly greet her with a warm reception, something like, "Hey, thanks for being on time. We appreciate knowing you're safe. Hope you had fun. I'm going to bed now, but when you're ready to log on tomorrow to order that new app you just earned, let me know and I'll type in my credit card number." Again, notice that the reward itself doesn't have to immediately follow the desired behavior, but as you're beginning to reinforce the behavior, you do need to immediately alert your child that she's on the right track. Be the slot machine that pays out a pellet to say, "Keep playing."

Despite my assurances that reward is the strongest branch in the Tree, many parents tell me they have any of four concerns about rewarding their kids. In case you share any of these concerns, let's address them before moving on to discussing the other branches in the Tree.

Concern #1: Isn't rewarding my kid the same as bribing him?

Reward is much different from bribery. By definition, a bribe precedes the behavior, while a reward follows it. And by some definitions, a bribe manipulates or coerces a person in a position of power to behave a certain way. A case could be made for using bribery to incentivize doing homework instead of playing a video game, but bribery is limitedly effective because when the prize precedes the work, the work is less likely to get done. (More about how to sequence responsibilities and privileges when we come to Step III.)

On the other hand, rewarding Junior with something he likes after he studies is appropriate and effective. It's a way of modifying the environment so that the choice to do something healthy and worthwhile, like studying, rivals the alternative choice of not studying (and doing something more pleasant instead, like playing the game). You're offering the proverbial second marshmallow in exchange for his delaying the gratification of eating the first.

Think of the distinction between reward and bribery this way: you go to work and then you get paid. You are being rewarded, not bribed, for going to work. Hopefully you are rewarded by your inherent enjoyment of your job also.

Certainly, even prizes that follow the work can be awarded irresponsibly, such as when they are awarded in response to misbehavior. An example would be unintentionally rewarding your daughter's tantrum by giving in and granting screen time.

But when you offer to give a reasonable incentive following your daughter's appropriate behavior, you are rewarding her in a healthy way that mirrors working an honest job and being awarded a fair payment for it, and you certainly do not need to worry that you're bribing her.

Concern #2: Is it appropriate or necessary for me to incentivize my child for something he should do anyway?

I agree that what your child "should" do, in the moral sense of the word *should*, is follow your instructions. That's one of his jobs. Wouldn't that be nice if he performed it consistently? While that would be ideal, it's not realistic. What your child "should"—and will—do in a psychological sense is seek pleasure. Activities your child finds immediately pleasurable are inherently rewarding. So expect that he initially will choose those activities over other more challenging activities whose rewards come later. That's why it's so important that you initially reinforce him immediately with a small marker of his progress toward the ultimate reward he's working for.

Junior is not yet going to grasp, let alone be motivated by, the idea that studying is the first important step (of about a zillion) toward earning his college diploma and becoming the successful businessman he wants to be—or, perhaps more accurately, that *you* want him to be. So instead of trying to appeal to an underdeveloped sense of logic and imagining that Junior possesses an overdeveloped ability to delay gratification, you are going to *involve* Junior by aligning the three pathways: verbally identify studying as the better choice in the long term (instruction), afford Junior frequent opportunities to observe you modeling similar behavior by delaying your own gratification when appropriate (modeling), and incentivize sound decision making, especially when it's tempting to choose otherwise (outcomes).

Then ready your instinct to Dodge Friendly Fire, because as part of the learning process, Junior may or may not choose the way you think he should. If he makes a shortsighted choice, you might have to get out of the house for some self-care as a means of protecting yourself from collateral damage as he learns by experience.

Concern #3: Once I start incentivizing a behavior, will my child be able to continue behaving even once I stop rewarding him? Didn't he just go through the motions to get the prize? I'm concerned he'll never grasp the

true value of the task.

Great point! In order to ensure that your child continues behaving even as you lessen the incentive you're offering, I would encourage you to issue rewards to jump-start your child's initiation of the desired behavior. Then, fade out those rewards as she begins to perform the behavior out of habit. This will occur right about the same time she finds the desired behavior inherently worthwhile due to the pleasant outcomes it naturally generates.

If the desired behavior begins to disappear as you fade out the rewards, then stay flexible. You might have to continue incentivizing the desired behavior a bit longer or invite your child to identify new rewards that motivate her until those occurring naturally begin to do the job of incentivizing the behavior for you.

The interplay between behavior and reward is constantly changing anyway, so no paradigm will last forever. As children mature, the ways they have fun change, and you redefine their responsibilities. The stakes get higher on both sides. Your daughter's desire for a trike evolves into her desire for a car, as your instruction to "keep your hands to yourself" evolves into your instruction to "keep your boyfriend's hands to himself."

Concern #4: It seems my child's only motivation is screen time. Is it okay to use something I'm trying to limit as an incentive?

Many parents point out that the only reward their child will find worth pursuing is screen time. That might turn out to be true, but before assuming it is, be sure to ask your child for a list of things that would motivate him. He might surprise you by generating a list of rewards that you find worthwhile, too. If he struggles to generate a list that you find acceptable, help him get started. Recall that the whole purpose of this book is to unplug and reconnect. Here are some low-tech activities that you and he can do together that you both might find rewarding, even if they are not as stimulating as enjoying screen time:

- Building a model
- Going to a museum
- Volunteering at a hospital
- Shooting baskets
- Playing a card game called Egyptian Rat Slap. Cards are boring? Not anymore. Since technology isn't inherently bad, type that game title into your browser and look up its rules. You'll find that the game is a lot more exciting than Go Fish, and so

it might just appeal to your kid (oh, and to you).

If it turns out that all Junior currently finds motivating is screen time, don't panic. In fact, most times you'll probably want to use it as an incentive, because doing so will advance the superordinate goal of helping Junior balance his jobs by sequencing his responsibilities ahead of his privileges. And rest assured you can use screen time as an incentive in ways that still match your values. We will discuss in detail how to do so when we come to Step III, but for now an analogy might help you decide the general approach you want to take in your particular situation.

Consider the difference between Western and homeopathic medicines. While each seeks the same ultimate goal of healing, the former attempts to do so by obliterating the pathogen, and the latter suggests that "like cures like," treating the pathogen with highly diluted doses of itself in order to stimulate the body's natural immune response.

Choose a Western approach to help Junior decide *not* to play by placing a game or movie off limits if you fundamentally oppose its content, or if Junior acts out or underperforms as a result of playing or watching it. If you approve of a game or movie's content and Junior is well behaved and high achieving, then choose a homeopathic approach that helps him learn *when* to play or watch by way of administering controlled doses of screen time in response to his making the tough choice to limit his screen time. In other words, you'll want to choose a homeopathic approach if Junior just needs a little help prioritizing home and school performance over screen time.

I hope that the preceding pages have assuaged any concerns you might have had about using reward to shape behavior, because I'm confident you'll find reward to be quite powerful. Let's discuss the second branch in the Tree and see if it might be useful to you as well.

Punishment

And now, on to punishment! Sound fun? Of course not. As shown in the Tree, basic punishment entails getting something painful, noxious, or unpleasant—something you don't like. Using punishment is punishing all around—you don't like punishing your child, and he doesn't like being punished.

I will concede that maybe losing your cool and lecturing your son felt like an outlet to you, but he tuned you out anyway. Your lecture didn't work. Or maybe while you were spanking your son, you temporarily prevented him from playing Xbox, but the threat of another spanking didn't stop him from sneaking the Xbox again later. Or even if it did, he resented you for threatening him out of doing what he likes—so he unplugged but he had no desire to reconnect.

In addition to being unpleasant for both parties, basic punishment is limitedly effective in deterring your child from seeking what he wants simply because punishment doesn't help him learn how to live without committing the problematic behavior. He still wants what he wants and can try to go get it once the punishment is over, if not sooner. Now his objective is to avoid the punishment while still seeking the reward. In addition to the fact that people seek pleasure, the other half of Freud's pleasure principle is that people avoid pain.

Basic punishment turns out to be a pretty weak branch in the Tree. Instead of imposing emotional or physical pain, the relatively more effective and pleasant way of de-incentivizing your kid from committing the problematic behavior is to arrange a paradigm in which the problematic behavior ultimately limits what he wants. If the problematic behavior costs him the very thing he wants, then he has an opportunity to learn to stop responding that way and to choose to behave appropriately instead (so that he gets what he wants). The second-strongest branch in the Tree is the one leading to response cost.

Response Cost

Response cost is a variant of basic punishment, but is different from it in a simple but important way: as shown in the Tree, response cost is the outcome when your behavior limits something you like. As people, we want what we want and don't like losing out on it. So if we know a behavior (i.e., a response) costs too much, we don't do it. As such, response cost can be a powerful deterrent to misbehavior. Response cost and reward are effective because they leave the person with plenty of control: you can choose to behave in ways that get you what you want and in ways that allow you to keep it. Along with leaning on the reward branch to incentivize Junior's appropriate behavior, you'll want to lean on the response cost branch to de-incentivize his inappropriate behavior.

Response cost is a necessary evil that occurs naturally within the process of pursuing your ultimate goal. Response cost is kind of like a built-in reality check. You might sometimes decide that response costs are worth incurring, such as when you decide to go into debt to buy a house, despite the interest you'll have to repay. But if you know ahead of time that the response cost is not worth it, you don't typically bother to incur it. Financing a mansion would get you a house that you like, but you'd never be able to travel anywhere. You'd be house-poor. You *can* choose to do it—the bank will probably allow you. (Heck, they'd love it if you owed them for life.) But you choose not to finance the mansion because it's not worth it. The cost of such a response is too expensive. It costs you the lifestyle you want even if it gets you the house.

Kids and adults alike typically react to response costs with mixed feelings because hitting the limit and knowing where the edge is can be reassuring but frustrating. The 110 Freeway just south of Pasadena, California, is one of the oldest stretches of highway in the country. And it shows. There's virtually no shoulder, and the only thing separating northbound traffic from southbound is a metal guardrail with wooden guideposts. I love and hate that guardrail. I am grateful for its existence for obvious reasons, but without a shoulder, the guardrail is uncomfortably close to the left side of the car. I know where the limit is, and so do my fellow motorists driving in the opposite direction. I wish the guardrail wasn't there so I could have just a little more room, but the result of its absence would be disastrous.

You can anticipate that your child will react with some resistance to encountering "the edge" of what is tolerated in your home. On the other hand, you can expect your child to react with subtle indications of reassurance at learning that the adults are ultimately in charge and that there are rules that make things more safe, fair, and predictable. You can expect your daughter to show some signs that she is grateful that you're willing to help her set limits on her screen use, because your doing so implies that there are more important things in our lives than our tech devices or our pleasure. Additionally, that the adults are in charge is part of what helps your daughter stay appropriately dependent on you and willing to consult with you. In short, your being in charge, including orienting her to realistic response costs, is part of what keeps her connected with you.

A teenager I see at my office is in the process of reconciling his mixed feelings about response cost with regard to his use of his smartphone. He recently referred to his beloved phone as a "black hole." He really enjoys using it, but he recognizes that his enjoyment sometimes sucks him into a longer engagement than he had planned. He both appreciates and resists working with me on setting limits that help him stop using the phone before doing so eats up too much of his time. For example, setting a timer (even if he does so on the phone) or asking a sibling to nudge him in ten minutes orients him to the passage of time. And keeping handy a list of fun, tech-free activities like taking a jog, practicing magic tricks, or reading a vintage comic book reminds him that choosing to turn off the phone certainly isn't choosing boredom over fun. We are working on helping him shift to a thought process that explicitly reminds him of rewards and response costs, such as, *Choosing to unplug is choosing fun in ways I don't later want to regret having let pass me by.*

Let's consider how response cost might be operating within your home when it comes to your child's overreliance on technology. For example, what's Junior's response cost for playing the video game instead of studying?

Is the response cost that you, his parent, are yelling at him? Nope; that's the punishment he tries to escape. That's the unpleasant outcome that comes with playing the game instead of studying.

Is the response cost the pleasure he experiences when he plays? Nope; that's the reward, and his pleasure is why he keeps playing even if he can't escape your yelling at him.

What's the response cost, what's the thing that he loses out on as a function of playing the game?

Nothing.

He loses out on nothing (that he's aware of—remember, he's currently satisfied with his virtual relationships), so he would simply rather play than not. Smart kid. Keep playing, Junior! The adults haven't figured out how to motivate you to make an even smarter choice—yet.

I'm about to provide more concrete examples of how to use reward in conjunction with response cost. First, let's complete our discussion of outcomes by addressing relief.

Relief

As shown in the Tree, relief is the outcome when a behavior limits something you don't like. Relief is the removal—the "lifting"—of a basic punishment. For example, as a kid, you were relieved when your mom stopped spanking or lecturing you.

Relief's dialectic relationship with punishment reminds us why a strategy like lecturing Junior for gaming too much is not working. If all he has to look forward to by not playing the game is the relief of having you not lecture him, then he is going to keep playing the game. In fact, while your lecture might constitute a punishment, angering you to the point that you launch into the lecture is an additional reward to him because he's controlling your behavior. Think back to the Reverse Hierarchy, in which the game plays Junior and Junior plays you. Junior rather likes under-functioning and playing while you over-function and try to figure out how to get him to fulfill his tougher jobs. Relief is a relatively weak branch in the Tree.

Relief also does little to shape long-term behavior because it is not something you seek like you do a reward. Did you know that cocaine loses its addictive properties when its medicinal strain is administered gradually as an anesthetic to a hospitalized patient? The patient is relieved, not rewarded. Because he never achieves a high, he does not become dependent on or addicted to cocaine. And nobody volunteers to go back into surgery just so they can be administered more doses of medicinal cocaine.

Similarly, you don't hear someone say how excited he is to have gotten a headache because of how great it will feel to get rid of it. Alleviating pain doesn't feel as good as finding pleasure. Alleviating a headache is not as enjoyable as getting a caffeine buzz. That's why many of us are pretty hooked on caffeine but not on ibuprofen.

Certainly, some people also become addicted to painkillers taken at home, but that's because the term *painkiller* is a misnomer. When such drugs are narcotic-based, often they do not merely eliminate pain; they also immediately increase pleasure. They are both relievers and rewards! No wonder people get addicted. Again, what's the problem? Is the problem the person because he likes feeling good and dislikes feeling bad? I think not. Perhaps labeling these medications for what they really are would help warn the consumer. But I digress.

You get the point: To shape behavior with outcomes, rely primarily on the sturdier branches of reward and response cost. Avoid using the combination of basic punishment and relief.

The Pruned Tree

Since the reward and response cost branches can be thought of as the two stronger ones, let's prune the Tree so that only those two branches appear. Compared to the original Tree, the following represents an even simpler image to remember when you're shaping behavior by way of outcomes.

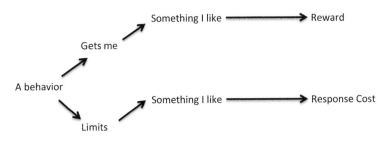

The Pruned Tree

I strongly encourage you to issue incentivizing rewards and expensive response costs until naturally occurring rewards and response costs take over the shaping of your child's behavior for you. A scenario from your adult life might help you get a sense of how to implement a paradigm of rewards and corresponding response costs for Junior. I'm a big fan of using real-world scenarios to help establish in-home behavior paradigms, because such arrangements afford your child practice at living by the same kinds of rules as those that govern the adult world.

Consider the rewards and response costs associated with your monthly utilities, like electricity. You want access to this magical force that offers light, air-conditioning, and power to your appliances. By your own volition, you work to get it. In short, electricity is a reward whose response cost is worth it. Basic punishment doesn't even factor into the equation: no one yelled at you to get you to want electricity. And if you don't pay your electric bill, no one comes over and lectures you. No one spanks you and then leaves you relieved when they stop. You just lose your electricity until you pay your bill, plus the service fees to turn it back on. The potential costs of losing your electricity and paying a higher bill, combined with the reward of enjoying electricity, make your choice to go to work and pay your electric bill a no-brainer.

Let's consider Junior's tech use in light of this scenario and discuss how you might implement a reward and response cost paradigm that will help Junior learn to make healthy choices too. Instead of lecturing Junior when he earns a C and then getting into a fight about screen time, simply ask Junior if he'd like to be in charge of his own screen time and other privileges. Spoiler alert: as your instinct to Dodge Friendly Fire will remind you, kids want to learn for themselves. So Junior will actually listen to your question, and he'll emphatically answer that he wants to be in charge.

Once you have Junior's attention, you can invite him to demonstrate how much control of his screen time and other privileges he is ready for by virtue of his home behavior and school performance.

After all, actions speak. To make this agreement concrete, invite him to draft a rider, just like his favorite musical artist does when contracting to perform at a given venue. The rider lists all the amenities the artist requests to have available backstage and in the dressing room. Ask Junior to jot down any items or privileges that would motivate him to demonstrate his finest behavior and performance.

Be prepared that Junior might not even agree to talk about drafting a rider. If that's the case, then notice an important clue hiding within the context: he probably finds the current arrangement to be skewed in his favor already, so he's not interested in doing anything that might change it. So tell him the current arrangement is off and his choice to not talk with you will limit his screen time and other privileges until he's ready to consider a new arrangement. The current arrangement being nullified is the response cost for his refusing to discuss a new arrangement.

Whenever Junior is sufficiently motivated to draft a rider, you might discover that he expects you to give him the moon in return for his shooting for it. "Well, Dad, you want me to get straight As, so I want to be able to use my phone anytime—day or night. Deal?" Hmmm. Not necessarily. That

particular rider might be fraught with problems—
an unrealistic academic goal, a risky and potentially
irresponsible way of using the phone, an emphasis
on what you both want instead of what actually
takes place. So instead of accepting the deal,
do some negotiating and whittle the rider down
so that it documents a realistic, appropriate, and
measurable exchange.

Wouldn't it be great if that were the approach
the venue took with the musical artist if it decided
the artist's requests on his rider exceeded the
expected value of his show? "I'm sorry, Mr.
Bieber. The way you behaved and performed last
time you were here resulted in a booing crowd
of people who might not return to your next
show. If we're not convinced that your show will
sell out our venue, then we're not interested in
meeting more of your lavish backstage 'needs.'
Why don't you draft a much less demanding rider
and propose a deal that offers some assurance
that your return will match our investment? For
example, perhaps for starters this venue can offer
you some water in exchange for your showing up
and taking the stage on time."

As you and Junior negotiate his rider,
remember to let him steer the conversation so
that it's all about Junior's behavior in relation to

what he wants, so he comes to care about how he behaves. You are gradually recalibrating the moral compass here. Start by matching a couple of your goals for Junior with a couple of his preferred ways of using tech. The conversation might sound something like this:

You: "Junior, you know how ever since we got you that new phone for your birthday, we've been fighting over when you can use it?" *(You describe the problem as being shared between you and external to both of you. You also preempt an argument about who the phone's true owner is.)*

Junior: "Um, yeah. Obvsies. I hate that you do that. It's mine, you know." *(Junior can be ill tempered at times, can't he? That's part of bein' a kid—don't sweat it.)*

You: "Well, you're right. It is yours. I won't be taking it away from you, so we won't waste time arguing about that. But I will need to put your phone plan on hold or cancel it entirely until you earn any further talk time or texts. With your grades tanking and the way you've been talking to your mom, I'm not convinced that you can handle using it whenever you want. But ultimately, and hopefully soon, I want you to have the control over when you use it. I think that's what you'd like too." *(You stay focused on the solution and its mutual benefit. You also continue to do a nice job of avoiding an unnecessary argument over phone ownership. Who cares if Junior insists he owns a phone when it's been rendered useless because you no longer pay for its plan?)*

Junior: "Duh!"

You: "Then show us how responsible you are, and that's how much talk time and texting I'll pay for on your phone."

Junior: "Like, by doing my homework?" *(He senses you're being reasonable, so he's starting to participate with more genuine interest.)*

You: "Sounds great. How about for every assignment you complete and turn in on time, you get five texts. I'll monitor your phone use to be sure you don't exceed your earned texts. When you consistently spend fewer than you've earned for a couple of months in a row, then I'll start to monitor less and I'll even pay for more. But, if you spend more than you've earned, you'll be showing me you're not ready for this kind of arrangement, and we'll have to try a deal that doesn't involve any private phone use." *(You start with a realistic,* *appropriate, and measurable exchange that clearly outlines the rewards and response costs.)*

Junior: "That's a start. But I want more than that." *(I recognize that he's being snarky within this example and that you don't want to reinforce that kind of attitude, but if part of how he responds is to ask for more time and texts, then great! He's inviting you to help him identify ways that he can earn them. Maybe you suggest that one way to earn them would be to speak more respectfully.)*

You: "Okay, what else do you want?" *(You let him identify what would motivate him, and you let him care more than you do about earning the bonus.)*

Junior: "Well you said you have a problem with how I've been talking to Mom. So, fine, I'll be respectful. But I want to be able to get talk time and buy apps." *(He's on the right track, but he's asking you to grant these privileges in exchange for his promising to be more respectful, not in exchange for his having done so already. Actions speak, and you're not interested in offering a bribe. Also, you need a way of measuring his degree of respect. So you'll want to respond in a way that both establishes how the abstract concept of respect will be measured and ensures that the responsibility* *precedes the reward. We will cover in detail how to measure abstract behavioral concepts and how to order responsibilities and privileges when we come to Step III.)*

You: "How about every time I hear you talking to Mom respectfully, I'll count one tally. A five-dollar app or five minutes of talk time will cost you twenty tallies." *(All of you will enjoy Junior's earning rewards following his speaking respectfully. No more arguments following his speaking disrespectfully because everyone will know the deal.)*

Junior: "Um, okay." *(He's a little less snarky by now.)*

You: "Let's try this for a week and see how it goes. Why don't you jot down the details so we both remember what we've agreed to."

Notice that the initial arrangement isn't set in stone. Rather, you are just trying a new paradigm of rewards and response costs to see if it works better than the old one. Instead of your son begging for his phone, neglecting his homework, and snapping at his mom, you want to see if he'll begin to "rebel" in a much more pleasant way—by really sticking it to you via racking up phone time and text messages he knows you have to pay for.

How do you find or arrange a plan that allows you to pay only for what he earns? There are several options. You might sign up for a flexible phone plan with a service like Ting, and put the plan into Junior's name. At the end of the month, you pay only for the minutes and texts his behavior at school and home has earned. Junior has to either responsibly limit his own talk time and texts or earn the money necessary to pay the rest of his bill (by behaving responsibly in other ways, like getting a job or completing paid chores around the house), or Ting will cancel his contract and he will be stuck with any cancellation fee.

Alternatively, maybe you sign up for a prepaid plan, where the amount you prepay for in the coming month is determined by Junior's behavior during the preceding month. The better his behavior, the more time and texts you prepay for.

A third option would be to sign a phone contract on Junior's behalf, and impose any necessary limits on the use of the phone yourself. In such a scenario, you can avoid getting into a tug of war for the device and simply list the act of turning it in when the earned amount of minutes or texts has been spent as one of the behaviors necessary to maintain further use of the phone. If Junior perpetually refuses to turn it in on time or continually exceeds his talk and text budget, you can cancel the plan and bill Junior for the cancellation fee you paid on his behalf. Start by asking Junior to pay you back the fee. If he refuses, you can impose further response costs simply by reallocating monies you might otherwise have granted him for recreational activities. For example, you can elect not to help him finance that upcoming trip to the amusement park and count the savings toward the cancellation fee you just covered.

If you have to cut the plan, don't waste time and energy feeling guilty. In actuality, he cut it. You didn't take away the phone. Instead, you wisely decided to finance only what his behavior warranted, and you thereby helped him encounter real-world limits like those he'll face in college, at his job, with his credit card company, and on the 110 Freeway.

And what if the opposite scenario plays out—Junior racks up a ton of time and texts on his plan, yet nonetheless fulfills his school and home responsibilities? Then the rider worked. Problem solved. He's figured out how to balance fun with school and home—he's figured out how to balance the three jobs of being a kid! Don't panic and refuse to grant him the time and texts he's earned. Reward him for it!

In such a scenario, studying sufficiently and speaking respectfully in order to enjoy plenty of phone use has become a no-brainer for him, just as going to work to pay for your electricity is for you. As Junior finds balancing his jobs becoming self-reinforcing, he can redraft his rider so it pertains to new responsibilities and privileges. Over time, you'll likely find that the riders can become less formal and explicit so that by the time Junior leaves for college (and hopefully before), he's established the practice of motivating himself by having identified the rewards and response costs inherent to any given task.

★ ★ ★

Aligning the Three Pathways

To close out the chapter, let's review the three pathways to learning and the importance of aligning them by reviewing two very different deliberations your child could undergo. These examples are meant to represent opposite ends of the continuum of possibilities. In each of them, see if you can identify the orientation of the hierarchy, whether the parents are unified, and the role of the screen. Try to label who is doing the playing and who is being played. Notice broader themes, such as true engagement with others vs. pseudo-engagement. Consider the condition of the water in the metaphorical fishbowl.

In the first scenario, things have gotten really bad. The three pathways to learning are perpendicular, and punishment and relief are the primary branches being relied upon. Your child's inner decision-making process could then understandably sound something like this:

Dad's such a hypocrite! He tells me to quit going to those sites on my laptop, when I caught him going to the exact same ones! Who cares what I watch? Plus, if he catches me, all he does is yell at me . . . kinda like Mom does to him. But it's pretty fun to see him get all worked up about catching me do something he gets in trouble for too. Plus, if I act real sorry, he stops yelling, then he just hides my laptop until I find it when he leaves for work. My conclusion? **It was worth it. I'll do it again.**

Smart kid, in that his thought process makes sense given his environment. To an extent, each parent's behavior is understandable too: one is dissatisfied at some level with the other, with Dad coping by looking at porn and Mom expressing herself by yelling. The problem doesn't belong to any one member. Rather, this family is thinking and behaving exactly as we would expect them to in such a polluted fishbowl.

At the opposite end of the continuum, here's the ideal thought process that your child might have in such a situation. This scenario will sound unrealistic, but it represents what you're shooting for. And, if you align all three paths and rely heavily upon reward and response cost, it even might be feasible:

Hmmm. My staying off these sites is so important to my parents that they sat down together with me and delivered one message: the women on the sites are being treated as objects, they are being paid for appearing, and the situations are unrealistic. My dad told me those are the reasons he doesn't bother with these sites. I think I believe him. I overheard a few of the other dads invite him to the strip club after my baseball game, but he said no and came out to dinner with the team and the rest of the dads. That was pretty cool, I guess, even though his jokes at dinner were lame. Then again, maybe he didn't find it that hard to avoid the strip club because he and Mom seem pretty content together. But how am I supposed to be expected to avoid these sites? I don't even have a girlfriend. Man, I want one, though . . . like my new lab partner in science. She's so hot. What was the name of that one site again?

Wait a minute. My parents said every time they check my browser history and it's clean, they are going to give me an iTunes gift card. I definitely want some of those. Plus, every time they check the history and it's not clean, I am only allowed to use the laptop in the kitchen for the rest of the week! That would suck. And they really do know how to check whether I've just deleted my browser history and emptied my cache. My conclusion? **Maybe I'll try keeping the browser history clean, and I'll use my gift card to buy my lab partner her favorite song.**

Smart kid. His behavior makes a lot of sense, too. His parents are doing a superb job. They understand they will place him in a difficult position if they merely instruct that he inhibit the natural impulse to visit inappropriate sites. They know he would struggle greatly to inhibit such a response without at least a competing reward and the possibility of encountering a cost if he doesn't. As such, they're facilitating the wise choice he wouldn't otherwise have the self-control to make. They're helping him calibrate his moral compass. The fishbowl is pretty clean, and there's a *lot* floating around that the kid will use in his own family's ecosystem someday.

But the second scenario sounds almost too good to be true, doesn't it? For example, the kid seemed to respond to the reward his parents offered and the response cost they issued. (In case you didn't catch the response cost, it was the loss of independent laptop use. Their rule that he moves the laptop to the kitchen would only constitute a basic punishment if they introduced an unpleasant outcome, like badgering him until he did so.)

How did the parents know which reward to offer? The kid listed it on his rider and the parents also paid attention to what the kid's actions bespoke about what would motivate him.

How did they know which response cost to issue? They explored the context for clues. Their kid was visiting inappropriate sites while in isolation, so it was reasonable to suggest he come out of isolation if he couldn't stay off the sites on his own.

But what else did they say or avoid saying in the conversation they had with him? What would they have done if he had threatened them when they tried to lay the ground rules? And how do they check his browser history if he clears the cache? The remaining chapters will answer these questions by deepening your understanding of the solution and how to implement it in your home.

Chapter 4

What Not to Say . . .
and What to Say Instead

"The limits of my language mean the limits of my world."
—Ludwig Wittgenstein

The philosopher Ludwig Wittgenstein understood that how we mentally frame things depends on the language we use, and that our framing then influences how we react. We set our own limits by how we describe things to ourselves. Wittgenstein understood the same truth that every obstetrician does: the delivery is really important.

We learned as children how to describe things to ourselves by listening to how the adults described things to us (and to themselves). As a child, it's hard to hear an instruction, hold on to it, and adopt it—even if it's true—if the delivery gets in the way of the message, like if you text your kid an instruction to "quit texting for the night." The ways we pose paradigms for our kids translates directly into the permanence and success of those paradigms.

But it's difficult to say the right thing in the right way to your kid about so many topics, most certainly including your family's screen problem. And it's really easy to say the wrong thing. This chapter identifies several common words and phrases that you'll want to avoid, as well as some more effective alternatives. As you read, see if you can spot the inherent allusions to observation, instruction, and the use of rewards and response costs as outcomes.

"Should"

Sarah Jessica Parker's character on *Sex and the City* was a blogger named Carrie. In one of her blogs, she questioned, "Why are we *should*-ing all over ourselves?" Carrie is also the name of my favorite psychologist—my wife, the other Dr. Dilley in our private practice.

My Carrie knows from plenty of clinical and personal experience how important it is that we parents choose our words carefully, and she agrees with the TV Carrie: *should* is a term that is limitedly useful. *Should* can help gauge the moral imperative, as in, "I should not kill that person who cut me off in traffic." Or, more domestically, "My son really should put his phone on the charger and go to sleep."

But in a psychological, physical, and philosophical sense, what "should" happen is what *does* happen and what you thus *can expect* to happen. In a just world, we shouldn't have earthquakes that claim lives. But the laws of physics necessitate that when plates in Earth's crust move, so do the things that rest atop them by virtue of gravity. The result is—*has* to be, and by this definition *should* be—some degree of destruction. If things were right and just in a moral sense, children would always listen to their parents' rules about technology. But as was discussed in the last chapter, what children do is seek pleasure and avoid pain. And consider our context. In the world we occupy, even healthy development includes testing limits. Children should sometimes test limits, especially about a privilege that's as tantalizing as tech use, precisely because that's what maturing children do.

So rather than setting unrealistically high expectations about what should be, or getting distraught over the fact that there is a gap between the ideal and the real when it comes to your kid and his tech, the task is to treat the gap as a given and to anticipate that you'll encounter it from time to time. Some alternatives to "you should" include "I wish that you would . . ." or "It would be great if we all could . . ." Notice that you're conjuring for your child images of what you want things at home to look like, without overt pressure to *make* things look that way or expressing disappointment that they presently look differently.

In one of my favorite books on optimizing performance, *The Inner Game of Tennis: The Classic Guide to the Mental Side of Peak Performance*, author W. Timothy Gallwey captures these sentiments as follows:

> When we plant a rose seed in the earth, we notice that it is small, but we do not criticize it as "rootless and stemless." We treat it as a seed, giving it the water and nourishment required of a seed. When it first shoots up out of the earth, we don't condemn it as immature and underdeveloped; nor do we criticize the buds for not being open when they appear. We stand in wonder at the process taking place and give the plant the care it needs at each stage of its

development. The rose is a rose from the time it is a seed to the time it dies. Within it, at all times, it contains its whole potential. It seems to be constantly in the process of change; yet at each state, at each moment, it is perfectly all right as it is.

Many athletes read Gallwey's books to enhance performance. When parenting is what you're performing, your child is the rose who doesn't find your disappointment helpful to her growth, but rather seeks your care and approval. Something like, "You're going to make a great choice about turning that off" will always appeal more to your child than, "You should know better than to keep watching that."

"I'm taking it away!"

This might sound like a semantic difference, but it's critical that you not "take away" screens from your child, but rather that your child "lose access" to them temporarily (because his misbehavior limits what he likes). You don't want your child to resent you; you want him to know whether you think he's ready to handle the privilege at hand and, if he's not ready, what the response cost is. That's how the rider works. You don't start taking away minutes and texts when he underperforms; rather, he simply doesn't earn as many as he'd like.

Use a "When you___, then you___" construction. Let's say that you bought Junior a phone and let him use it independently, then found out he was using it to send explicit messages to his female friends. Issue a response cost and tell him you thought he was ready for his own phone, but sexting would suggest that he's not. Assure him that *when* he shows you he's ready for a smartphone by virtue of safer social exchanges on a simple, low-tech phone, *then* you'll help make sure he gets rewarded with a smartphone. Instead of sounding like a nagging adult who doesn't "get it" and would prefer simply to take things away, you are foreshadowing the sales rep he'll someday work with when he buys his first luxury car: "I want to get you in this car today. But to do so, I need to show my underwriter that you established a strong credit history when you were paying for your old car."

Costco seems to have this phrasing mastered. A sign in the parking lot reminds shoppers to "keep your costs down" simply by returning their carts. How much more effective is this signage than one that reads, "If you don't put your cart back, we will take it away next time!" The chosen sign simply highlights how the system works without implying a threat. You can choose to return your cart and keep prices as low as possible for everyone. Or you can leave your cart dangling on the median—but at checkout next time we might all pay a few cents more for that zombie apocalypse-sized jug of salsa.

"Because I said so!"
Since we know that one of the ways kids learn is through observation, it follows that part of how kids develop deductive reasoning skills is to watch their parents use these skills. You might feel irritated when your child asks why, but she might be asking because she honestly doesn't see your rationale. If you try to explain your rationale and she doesn't want to listen, then, of course, don't feel like you have to continue to offer one. You can ignore the incessant questioning (how to do so effectively will be detailed in the next chapter) or issue response costs for her continuing to ask. But if she truly wants to know and is open to hearing your reasoning, then go ahead and offer it.

If the only rationale you provide for asking her to turn off the tablet, for example, is "Because I said so!" then there are two potential problems: First, you might *not* have a logical reason, and perhaps your position merits revision. Second, you might have a completely valid reason, but by withholding it and dismissing your child with "Because I said so!" you are inadvertently modeling the practice of emotional reasoning. Emotional reasoning is doing what you feel, independent of logic. If your child's understanding of your rationale is simply that you said so, then it's likely she'll conclude you decided what you did simply because you felt like it.

The solution is to share the thought process that drives your rationale. Even if your child doesn't like the answer, she will have observed you modeling sensibility and logical reasoning. Moreover, being welcomed into your thought process is part of how you connect; it's part of how she grows to trust you.

My dad is a psychologist who served as my first inspiration to become one myself. Growing up, he was really open to sharing his rationale underlying various house rules. I certainly disagreed with the rules on many occasions, but I typically understood his rationale, just as he listened to and understood mine. That mutual understanding helped us stay connected even when we disagreed, and by responding to my asking why instead of shutting it down, he encouraged me to stay curious about plenty of other things. What career would I have chosen had he dismissed my curiosities? Certainly not one whose basis is the question of why!

As a psychologist, I interact regularly with a colleague across the San Gabriel Valley who encourages parents to stay mindful of the reality that their children will soon be fully functioning adults in their twenties. She tells parents to "talk to your daughter now as the twentysomething she'll soon be." Kids are incredibly capable of understanding (though they will not necessarily agree with) their parents' rationales. Instead of "Because I said so!" what if you shared your thought process as though your child were already in her twenties? Isn't she more likely to find you approachable and respectful of her burgeoning independence, even if you have to maintain your limits?

Here's one example of how it might sound to talk with your child in such a way: "I asked you to turn off the tablet because I love you and want you to get enough sleep tonight so that you enjoy your field trip tomorrow. The fact that you're arguing with me about it right now suggests that maybe you didn't get enough sleep last night, when I let you stay on your tablet a little later than usual. By going with the flow and turning it off now, you'll be showing me that letting you stay up last night didn't create a domino effect after all and that you're not so dependent on this thing. Then maybe it will make sense for you to use it again tomorrow after you act responsibly on your field trip. But if you keep pushing back right now, what else can I conclude but that you didn't get enough sleep, so you need more right now, and you probably will need more tomorrow night too?"

Your gut told you technology stimulates, and you followed it. You're already right. When asked "Why?" don't be intimidated and disconnect. Confidently share and connect!

"You can't"

Do you hear the difference between "You can't use your phone until you finish your homework, and then it'll be bedtime anyway" and "As soon as you finish your homework, you can use your phone until bedtime"? The distinction is subtle, but the latter sounds more appealing, doesn't it? The latter extends plenty of control to your child, leaves open the possibility that he will finish his homework in advance of bedtime, and orients him to the fact that there's a reward to be had for doing so.

Imagine ordering your favorite entrée at your favorite restaurant and having your server reply, "You can't order that. It's eighty-sixed." You would much prefer he say, "You have great taste! So many people have ordered the grilled salmon tonight that we have run out. The pan-seared halibut is another popular option, if you're in the mood for seafood." You, the diner, maintain a considerable degree of control, and your server is going to help you find a great dish even though your first choice isn't available.

What the restaurant analogy does not offer is a reminder that starting a phrase to your child with "You can't . . ." is also an inadvertent way of putting ceilings on his dreams. If you think that this observation sounds extreme, recall Wittgenstein's quote. Why put the limit in your child's head? "You can't this," "You can't that"—kids hear these kinds of statements a lot as it is. They are already told they can't:

- Eat that dessert
- Stay up so late
- Sleep so late
- Sit in the front seat, much less drive
- Play at that friend's house
- Have that friend over
- Talk to their neighbor during class
- Leave the classroom
- Go off campus

And now, one more thing they can't do, and it pertains to their favorite habit: accessing the screen. To many kids, it can feel like the whole world is telling them all the things they can't do. You can see why they tune in to their devices and tune out parents!

The antidote is to shift into a "When you____, then you____" construction again. Don't reinvent the wheel. This construction works because it's fair and empowering. Instead of "You can't play that thing right now! What are you, crazy? We have guests coming over!" you'll want to say, "As soon as your room is clean for our guests, you are welcome to get back on the Xbox for a while until they arrive." You could also incentivize logging off by adding, "And then, when they arrive and you turn it off without complaint to come join us for dinner, you will have earned fifteen minutes of bonus time to use after they leave, or to cash in tomorrow if they don't leave until late tonight." You could also orient your child to any of several response costs of continuing to play: "But if they arrive and you keep playing, then you'll be showing me you're unable to handle the privilege of playing before our guests arrive next time. I don't think you'll find doing that to be worth it, so make a good choice. I'm sure you will."

WHAT NOT TO SAY . . . AND WHAT TO SAY INSTEAD

Recall the concept of object permanence and also the advice of my crosstown colleague about talking to your child like she's a twentysomething. You want your kid to be at college one day with the words you chose now comprising her internal self-talk. Will you have told her "You can't" or "You can"? You, dear reader, *can* be your child's voice of opportunity instead of limitation. Instead of, *I've been told what I can't do all my life, but now I can finally choose for myself to go to the football game instead of studying. I can't possibly concentrate. I'm going to text my friends right now,* you want her to think, *When I finish studying, then I can easily text my friends to find out where to meet them at the football game.*

"Once you're eighteen, *then* you can_____"
Nothing magical happens at the stroke of midnight that officially ushers in your child's eighteenth birthday. Neurologically, the same amount of growth occurs during the twenty-four-hour period marking his birthday as it did the day prior. Only in a legal sense is your child suddenly recognized as an adult. Your next of kin is still a teenager, likely still living under your roof, going to the same school and/or maintaining the same job he did (or did not) yesterday. Recall the story

of the mother who taught her son how to call for pizza. He wouldn't have suddenly been capable of such things without instruction just because he'd turned the age of majority. And think back to the considerations involved in deciding whether to uphold privacy or ensure safety. In itself, your child's age is not necessarily one of the primary considerations.

So don't make eighteen the "set point" for everything, including technological allowances, lest the whole family anticipate a sea change that isn't going to happen right away. Instead, when your child asks you if he is allowed to do some novel screen-based thing like watch a graphic movie, ask yourself how functionally old or mature he is showing himself to be by virtue of fulfilling his responsibilities, as your Actions Speak instinct would suggest. As he gradually demonstrates increased degrees of maturity, gradually grant more latitude to make his own choices (as will be further detailed in Step III). How close your kid is to age eighteen whenever he first balances his jobs in this way is not directly relevant.

Notice that this revised definition of *readiness* that depends on maturity rather than age also allows for growth to occur at your child's own unique pace, which can be motivating to him.

Instead of looking forward to a magical day years in the future, he has all the control and can choose to activate more privileges sooner by virtue of acting more responsibly now.

"So what?"

In your wisdom, you can sometimes determine very quickly that what your child wants is no big deal in the scheme of things—but it's currently a big deal to her. You'll want a reply that's not as dismissive as "So what?"

When you ask your child to turn off the game immediately, she might respond, "But I'll die" (meaning that it will be Game Over for her on-screen character). It might come as a surprise that your child's concern in that regard is actually legitimate. Remember losing the office pool? Sure, it wasn't that big of a deal, but you didn't like it. How about that tennis match? And your alma mater's bowl game?

Typically, losing stinks for kids *and* adults. In Western society, we place an emphasis on winning. We are socialized into believing that the destination defines the whole journey. We learn that if you lose, then the game or ref must have "sucked," or worse yet, *you* sucked. It makes sense that your kid only gets more upset if you "so what" her loss. Instead, try validating her feeling by identifying with it. Resonate with her. Affirm that it's hard to lose, and let her in on the truth that you don't like it either.

You can defuse so much of your child's frustration by validating her, even before you help solve the problem. (By the way, that holds true with your partner as well. In fact, you'll definitely want to validate before you help solve the problem. Haven't you been told, "I want you to understand, not fix it!"?) Then, once the iron is cool, add some of the insights you have gleaned in your experience.

Of course, you'll have to believe what you're telling your child for her to buy it. Part of why it's difficult for parents to validate our kids in these situations is that we only have one supportive phrase when they lose, and we don't believe it ourselves: "It's not whether you win or lose, it's how you play the game." But what does *that* mean? Your kid doesn't know either, and she'll appeal to you for a deeper philosophy: "Do you mean it's about whether I play the game well? If so, then how can I tell how I played? By how I feel? Well, I feel like I played well, but I must not have if I freaking *lost*!"

Instead of offering a consolation prize that you don't value yourself, orient your child to the game's existence in a larger context. Tell her how the whole point of play is to enjoy the moment, not stake all of her enjoyment on the ideal result, whether that's winning or being able to play forever. Remind your child that what matters is participating wholeheartedly, mindfully, gratefully in every second we are granted on this planet. Sure, winning makes doing so a little easier, but in truth, the outcome of winning is not inherently richer than the outcome of losing.

Tell her that the entirety of the play experience, of which the final score is only a part, is as rich as you make it. Then further calibrate her moral compass by modeling that what you just said is true and go play something together that doesn't even require keeping score. Do yoga together, including the breathing and meditation. Take her to the hardware store, mutually choose a new paint color for her room, and then come home and get messy. You will have said, modeled, and experienced together a much deeper and satisfying truth about the meaning and purpose of play than dismissing a loss could ever convey.

"Okay, fine, you can watch TV—but only if you leave me alone!"

If your child pressures you for screen time and

you cave, you might temporarily get him off your back. Technology can be a sort of babysitter that frees up your time. However, by yielding after your kid begs, you will have inadvertently rewarded the exact behavior you wanted to eliminate: the begging. If you ultimately flex on your limit as a result of his begging, he will have learned (by virtue of reward) to beg again the next time your initial answer feels unsatisfactory. Instead, you might ignore the begging, issue a response cost for it, or try the broken record technique, gently repeating your answer: "No."

You might also try another approach, one that respects your child's intelligence. When he asks a second time, try saying, "I think you already know the answer," or "We've already talked about that." You can even orient him to the reality that your decision is final, and remind him, "No amount of begging is going to change my decision, so we might as well spend our time together doing something else." Then schedule some time to hang out together when you're available and when your kid has cooled down about the limits you've just set. Dig out the Frisbee and head outside for some catch. Or pick up a gardening book, thumb through it, and plant a couple of crops in the backyard or a few herbs in the kitchen. Maybe go visit Grandma or find that gift card to the coffee shop and grab a couple of hot chocolates.

"Promise me you will sign out"/ "Do it for your mom"

I think one of the most underrated movies of the 1990s is Mike Myers's comedy *So I Married an Axe Murderer*. Part of why I'm a big fan can be explained by dry dialogue like the following exchange between Myers's character, Charlie, and his romantic interest, Harriet:

Harriet (evidently drawing their first date to a close): "It's late."

Charlie (hoping Harriet will agree to stay out with him): "Not for me."

Harriet: "Who for, then?"

Charlie (perplexed by Harriet's phrasing): "Who . . . for . . . then . . . what?"

For our purposes, the wry question "Who for then what?" can serve as a reminder that your child's screen time always has to matter more to her than it does to you. So make sure your kid knows that your request to have her sign out of Facebook when she's getting cyberbullied is more for her sake than yours. The alternative, begging your kid by saying things like, "Please promise me you'll sign out when I leave the room" or, "Please sign out. Do it for your mom. She does so much for you," fundamentally misses the point. These appeals are veiled guilt trips and thereby constitute low-intensity basic punishments.

Of course, such appeals sound well intentioned. But even if your child chooses to follow your direction, she is doing so for your benefit rather than grasping the rationale behind your request. Recall that basic punishment is effective in limiting behavior only temporarily. Over time, her having complied without really understanding why you asked will breed resentment. She will become determined that as soon as she's in college, she'll stay on Facebook as long as she pleases. She has decided that your requests were arbitrary and her options were limited because she could either comply with them or feel guilty. Yuck.

Your more effective move would be to orient your child to why it benefits *her* to sign out. Remind your daughter whom signing out of Facebook is really "for then," as Mike Myers's Charlie would advocate: "You know, sweetheart, you don't have to put up with this. Kids who bully other kids that way might seem to be 'on top' right now, but that's because this is as popular as they're going to get. Unless they figure out how to get along with others, they're peaking. Don't join them in trying to act in a way that's untrue to yourself only to burn out now. Your whole journey looks different—you are on the way up. Hey, want to come make dinner with me? In fact, let's make that dish you loved when we tried it last week. We'll look up the recipe online."

With this type of guidance, you are appealing to her age-appropriate self-focus by orienting her to what's at stake for her in deciding to log off, and thereby helping her potentially make the good choice again later on, when you aren't physically around. And you're taking a holistic approach, modeling and offering the appropriate use of one screen to invite her away from the problematic use of another. You're wisely offering an alternative whose pleasure rivals that of the default choice. Most important, you are inviting her to connect with you in reality, while orienting her to the larger context of that reality, including how her trajectory remains promising in spite of some of her peers' actions.

"If you _____ every day for a month, then you can _____"

Parents commonly invite their kids into a reinforcement system that's bound to fail because it's structured like a strict workout regimen. Consider this statement: "Junior, if you have good behavior at school for thirty days, then I'll buy you that game." This kind of proposal represents a good attempt to use "When you____, then you____" phrasing, but there are two problems with it.

First, notice that the proposal subtly implies that your child might not succeed (because it uses "*if* you" instead of "*when* you"). Second, anytime you specify a continuous length of time for which a behavior has to recur to generate a reward, you remove any possibility for imperfection along the way. In the preceding example, if Junior lasts twenty-nine days, then crumbles partway through the final day of the contract, he doesn't get the game. That would be like scoring 29/30 on a quiz and getting an F. Or if Junior falters one week in, then he loses all motivation to complete the final twenty-three days of the arrangement.

Instead, make the paradigm something like, "When you earn high behavior marks at school for a *total* of thirty [nonconsecutive] days, then you will have earned that game, and we'll schedule a time to go buy it." That way, Junior can decide, by virtue of his actions, how quickly he obtains the reward. It might take him the minimal amount of time—thirty days—or it might take him a few months.

Like each of the paradigms in this book, arrangements in which a reward is obtained by way of consistent, but not necessarily consecutive, behavior are meant to replicate the way the real world is structured, and thereby prepare your child for success outside of your home. You want to make a million bucks in real life? Go for it. How long will it take you? To a large extent, you decide. Nobody is tracking whether you do everything perfectly for some set amount of time and then awarding you a lump sum. Rather, you earn chunks along the way, striving for a ratio of output to income that you find favorable.

Once Junior earns the reward, happily go get it with him. You might find ridiculous his decision to cash in on a game. But don't try to persuade him to buy something else that you find more worthwhile (unless you fundamentally oppose the chosen game's content, as described earlier). Congratulate him. He did it! By upholding your end of the deal in allowing him to cash in on what he pleases, you provide the space he needs to mature and become interested in other activities over time. He has to learn by experience that buying a game isn't necessarily the best way to spend his hard-earned money.

More important, make the whole event of going to get the game a really interpersonally connected experience. Get lunch together afterward and ask

Junior about his life. Expect awkward silences. Don't pry. Anticipate ebbs and flows in the stimulation and the intensity of the conversation. This is a real relationship you're cultivating here as you calibrate the moral compass. Finding out more about his life might end up requiring you to first tell him more about yours. In fact, it might mean showing him more than telling him.

So on your way home, take Junior somewhere you would go yourself that he might enjoy too. Stop by the record store and let him literally feel the vibration of the warm tones that only a record can produce. Show him some of the records you used to collect, back when every song on the album had to be good in order for you to buy it, because there was no convenient way to haphazardly skip tracks. He might be surprised to see that many of his favorite modern artists are now recording on vinyl, too. If you listened to CDs or tapes rather than records, which ones were your favorites? Might they be fun for you to collect on vinyl now? Maybe hunting down vinyl gems becomes a shared hobby for the two of you. Shared hobbies like collecting something together narrow the generation gap so that Junior less often cites the gap as the reason you don't "get" things about him, like how much he needs technology.

"Just wait until your father gets home!"

Do not threaten your child with some statement like, "Your father will be home soon, and just *wait* until I tell him that you refused to turn that off!" Threats like these only set up that other parent to be the Bad Cop and engender resentment toward him. Plus, when Bad Cop comes home and doesn't start issuing citations quite like you'd hoped, you resent him, too.

Instead, whether it means calling upon your partner when you need help or simply keeping the adults unified atop the hierarchy, the point is to make it easier on both parents by having each apply a little leverage. To make that work, you'll initially have to communicate quite a bit with your partner, then less so as your child starts to behave more consistently.

For example, jotting your partner a quick text before he gets home can set the stage for what to expect: "Honey, Junior's only earned 10 mins of screen x so far & he probly won't finish his HW in time to cash it in tonite. So if he claims he's done and has earned his full hr, be sure to check! Gotta run to that mtg. ILY!"

★ ★ ★

As you carefully choose what to say, remember that you're trying to help your child establish the habit of listening to you. So make yourself easy and uplifting to listen to. Sometimes, even when you've coordinated with your partner and you've both said the "right" things, your child will still seek technology in offensive ways. In anticipation of such instances, you need to learn how to play defense. Specifically, you need to know how to issue response costs in a consistent and effective fashion. In the next chapter, I will teach you how to play this tricky form of defense, which requires a calm demeanor on your part.

Chapter 5

Playing Defense

"Wisdom is always an overmatch for strength."

—Phil Jackson

As a player, Phil Jackson won the National Basketball Association (NBA) championship twice. As a coach, he won it a record eleven times, his combined total of thirteen an NBA record. Jackson recently became the president of the New York Knicks, continuing his legacy of success.

When Jackson coached the Chicago Bulls and the Los Angeles Lakers (two of my favorite teams based on where I've lived), I loved watching him answer questions during press conferences. His poise was incredible. The press would try to trip him up, get him to cough up a detail, make him give them something—anything—to run with. They would stir the pot by asking what he thought about one of his players feuding with a competitor—or even more salacious, a teammate. And Jackson would stay supremely calm. How did he do it? Jackson has practiced Zen meditation for decades, which I think also contributed to the success of his teams. So he would respond to the provocative question by pressing his index and middle fingers to his temple, apparently reminding himself that he fully expected loaded questions from the press, then reply dismissively with something like, "Boy, you guys are really desperate for a story, aren't you?"

The Four Levels of the Triangle Defense

More influential on the actual game of basketball than Jackson's pithy quotes was his invention of a brilliant scheme called the Triangle Offense—but your child is already being plenty offensive in his quest for screen time. What you might find helpful is some coaching about how to play defense.

In the last chapter, I alluded to ignoring certain problematic behaviors. But what can you do if ignoring doesn't work? And what can you do if your child's egregiously inappropriate behavior cannot be ignored? You need a reliable system for answering these questions and playing good *D*.

The Triangle Defense is your guide to setting limits by issuing response costs. Implement the Triangle Defense with the same poise Coach Jackson modeled in responding to the press.

As we discuss each level of the Triangle Defense, it will be helpful to mentally situate the Triangle itself within the Pruned Tree. Since the Triangle Defense is your guide to issuing response costs, the image of the Triangle belongs on the response cost branch. Think of the Triangle as the fruit at the end of that branch, like this:

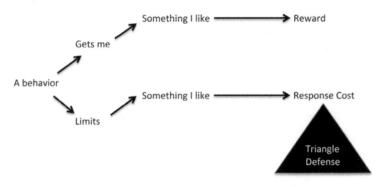

The Pruned, Fruit-Bearing Tree

Let It Go

When I was working on my doctorate at Northwestern University, I attended a group psychology conference in downtown Chicago. One of the more veteran therapists in attendance told a story about herself as a teen. She had done something that got her into trouble, and her mother told her she would not be able to attend the school dance. The therapist protested to her mother by screaming, "I hate you!" As she recounted the rest of the story at the conference, the therapist wept. Enamored of her mother's poise, she described how calm her mother had stayed, how she hadn't taken the bait, and how gently she had conveyed the bottom line to the therapist-to-be. Her mother had stoically replied, "Well, you're still not going." The therapist-to-be quickly recognized that expressing hatred was not going to change her mother's loving decision, or even alter the way her mother communicated its finality.

I wonder if a TV commercial producer was in attendance at the conference where my colleague told her story, because someone recently made an antidrug commercial that also compellingly demonstrates the calm but consistent way a parent might ideally respond to a child's provocation. The father is shown washing dishes and his adolescent daughter stands behind him, protesting that she should be able to go to an unchaperoned party. When her father continues to calmly deny her his permission, the daughter shouts that she hates him and stomps off . . . and he simply continues to wash the dishes.

In my Chicago colleague's story and in the TV commercial, the parents' responses depict ideal implementations of the bottom level of the Triangle Defense, Let It Go, which you'll want to use first and most frequently. Ideally, Let It Go is all that's necessary. When issuing response costs according to the Triangle Defense, the idea is to start at Level 1, stay there as long as possible, only elevate to Level 2 if necessary, and so on. Here's a close-up of Level 1 of the Triangle Defense.

The Triangle Defense, Level 1: Let It Go

In the preceding scenarios, the parents' understanding that paying attention to problematic behavior is part of what reinforces it, even if inadvertently, was crucial to the parents being able to simply ignore the intensity of the teens' statements. You can remember very easily what Let It Go means by considering how much you'd like to ignore the ubiquitous song from *Frozen* by the same name.

The parent who uses Let It Go might appear to the child to have lost the battle. In fact, however, the parent's non-response is a step toward winning the war. The child's provocative statement or offense did not gain undue attention or incite a big reaction. It encountered a stoic, logical parental response. Roman Catholic bishop St. Francis de Sales might have said it's the dispassionate nature of the parent's response that, ironically, gives it such force. He observed, "Nothing is so strong as gentleness, nothing so gentle as real strength."

So when your child acts out or tells you something provocative in an overt attempt to catch you off guard and push your buttons, the first course of action is to ignore the intensity of the behavior or statement by underreacting. Overmatch strength with wisdom.

It is imperative to note, however, that the old adage "Ignore it and it will go away" is not entirely accurate. It should really be "Ignore it and it will get worse, but keep right on ignoring it, and *then* it will probably go away."

The reason the behavior gets worse first, even when it is ignored—in fact, precisely because it is ignored—is due to a phenomenon called the Extinction Burst. The Extinction Burst is the last-ditch attempt to earn attention or obliterate the imposed limit. When parents continue to ignore the behavior *right on through* the Burst, the behavior typically extinguishes because the child decides to try something else (or stop trying altogether). Once even the most overstated version of the problematic behavior has failed to bring about the desired outcome, the child's recourse is usually to give up.

The next time you try letting go of a mild offense or plea and your child gets even louder or more insistent, rest assured: you're doing it right! Keep holding on, because the problematic behavior is on the verge of extinction. Extinction itself can be a process, with the intensity of each revised behavior waxing and waning, and ultimately becoming less offensive until more appropriate behaviors finally dominate.

As I write this, I am returning from a funeral of a distant family member, my brother-in-law's *ya-ya* (a Greek term for *grandmother*), who lived to nearly ninety-seven years old. On the backside of the funeral program were "shared little truths" that Ya-Ya used to say frequently. One said, "Don't gunny-sack—we aren't meant to carry these things around. They only weigh us down. Let it go!" Ya-Ya was right on, and I wonder if maybe letting go of these kinds of things is part of what allowed her to live for so long.

Here's a recent example of how I relied on Let It Go with *Frozen*'s number-one fan, my daughter. After dinner, she ate a cookie and then asked for another one. When I said, "No, honey," she protested. I ignored the protest. She grew louder. I continued to ignore the escalation. Once she realized she wasn't getting my attention and fell silent for a split second, I rewarded her taking pause by immediately granting her my attention and thanking her for having stopped begging—I paid out a little nugget of reinforcement like a slot machine does. Then I gently explained that one cookie was enough and reminded her how much she had enjoyed it. Fortunately, I was not devouring multiple cookies myself, or my modeling wouldn't have matched my instructions or outcomes. She nonetheless protested again, but more quietly than when she initially had done so. I breathed a sigh of relief, noticing that the protest had hit its ceiling and was inching toward extinction.

Encouragingly, Let It Go carried a preventive

effect. More recently, my daughter ate a cookie and asked politely for a second one, and I said, "No, not right now, sweetie." And that was it. She didn't protest or escalate. She had learned by way of instruction, modeling, and outcomes that acting out wouldn't earn her a second cookie. Then, to solidify the learning that had taken place, I rewarded her appropriate response with a sugar-free jackpot of praise and extra playtime before her bath.

The preceding example sounds pretty ideal. I offer it because it's a sleek depiction of how we all want such exchanges to go. They don't always go that way, though, including for us parents who are also mental-health professionals. And these situations become especially difficult when kids ask for just a *piece* of the proverbial cookie. Your child will probably try to get you to agree to just a bit of screen time here and there by saying, "Can't I just play for five minutes? Just five little minutes?" Keep it simple. Refer back to his rider. Your answer will be obvious to you both before you even put it into words. He has either earned five minutes of screen time by virtue of fulfilling some of his other jobs or he hasn't. If he hasn't, you can ignore him if he continues asking for "just five minutes." That should extinguish his continuing to ask (but expect him to initially ask even more or louder after you begin ignoring him).

I should mention that there *are* times when Let It Go just doesn't work, even after the Extinction Burst. But take heart, there is a reason for this too. Look around and investigate context. Often there is something less apparent reinforcing the problematic behavior: The child is having fun doing whatever the thing is, and it's still fun even if you ignore it and they don't get your (negative) attention. For example, ignoring the fact that your son hasn't turned off his phone is unlikely to get him to turn off his phone.

Perhaps equally as often, there are other explanations for why Let It Go doesn't necessarily work immediately or at all. Twelve-step recovery programs use the acronym HALT as a reminder not to let oneself become too Hungry, Angry, Lonely, or Tired, because these feeling states are triggers for making unhealthy choices. So too, your child might have become too *H*, *A*, *L*, or *T*, and until he recalibrates, his behavior can remain pretty volatile. Your task then is to stay curious about the problem in context. Look for clues.

Explore the details of the environment: Is there an overriding feeling state trumping your attempts to extinguish the behavior by letting it go? If so, address that feeling state first. Determine what's influencing his behavior even more than his desire for your attention. Get your child's blood sugar back up when he's too hungry, for example. Then, if necessary, implement the Triangle Defense again, starting over with Let It Go.

Chill Time

If Let It Go doesn't work or can't work because a behavior requires your immediate attention, then it's time to actively help your kid calm down. For example, if two siblings fight over a controller and it's going to get violent if you don't step in, your response is to elevate to Level 2 and issue Chill Time.

The Triangle Defense, Level 2: Chill Time

Chill Time often takes the form of a time-out. I like using a phrase like "go chill out for a minute" or "take a break" instead of "take a time-out," because time-out can carry a negative connotation. It doesn't matter what you call it, as long as your label is accurate and your kid knows what you're instructing him to do. What you're encouraging your kid to do at Level 2 is spend between two and five minutes relaxing in solitude without access to anything enjoyable (whether your attention or a Lego set). Doing so is not a basic punishment—you aren't applying pain in any form. In fact, when I remind parents in my office of the notion that Chill Time is not a basic punishment, they often respond by agreeing, "Yeah, it's a reward! I *wish* someone would encourage *me* to take a few minutes to myself just to take deep breaths and settle down!"

In addition to being a reward in some respects, Chill Time is a response cost because it limits whatever problematic thing your kid was doing that he liked as well as any alternatives (whether problematic or not) that he would also like. If he snaps at you while watching a movie on the iPad and doing so temporarily halts his movie while he chills out, he's less likely to snap at you next time.

Precisely how many minutes of Chill Time your child needs depends on the severity of his misbehavior and the time it takes him to calm down, but you're generally issuing a brief response cost of a few minutes here. There's no sense in assigning a twenty-minute time-out or relegating your son to his room for the weekend. The point of Chill Time is to calm down, not take a vacation from one another.

Certainly there are times to take longer breaks and even vacations from one another, but doing so when only a Level 2 response is warranted will engender confusion and resentment. You don't want your child thinking, *Geez, all I did was say something snarky to my mom—I don't even remember what—and I haven't been allowed to leave my room all day.* Assigning such a strong response cost isn't teaching much of a lesson, because your child isn't clear which of his behaviors generated the severe outcome. Further, unless you provide clarification, the confusion will eventually grow into anger. Unless that anger is resolved, it becomes resentment. Confusion, anger, and resentment are not feelings that facilitate reconnection.

Think back to the antidrug commercial. Notice that the daughter escalated up to Level 2 of the Triangle Defense and can be said to have put herself in Chill Time: she stomped off

THE GAME IS PLAYING YOUR KID

into her own space—into her own time-out of sorts—because her father didn't award any extra attention to the provocative statement. The father only needed to respond at Level 1, and his daughter self-imposed Level 2.

If you have to impose Chill Time, start with two minutes. If your child protests or takes the two minutes but hasn't calmed down, issue a third minute, and so on, up to about five minutes of Chill Time. If your child simply won't even start to chill out, or if he takes a full five minutes but is still out of control, it's time to move to Level 3 of the Triangle Defense.

Oregon Trail

When I was in grade school during the 1980s, students occasionally had the opportunity to use an Apple IIe computer, and if we were lucky, we even got to play a game that was considered pretty high-tech called Oregon Trail. The game depicted horses and settlers traversing the Northwest and trying to survive various plagues and predators. The settlers' conditions were about as primitive as how we would now regard the game's graphics: not high-tech at all!

In that sense, the game was true to life: In the days of the first American settlers, there were no electronic distractions, simply because there was no electricity. There were no reports of children watching violent TV shows and then acting violently themselves, because there was no TV. There wasn't even radio. Sure, kids and adults in those days got out of hand, at times from watching someone else model a loss of control. But whatever the cause of any aberrant behaviors committed by our pioneering ancestors, it wasn't watching hours of questionable behavior on a TV or completely vegging out on a tablet or phone.

Small wonder that a few days or even hours without electronics can be enormously calming and refreshing for adults and children alike. Taking such a hiatus from technology is what I refer to as "hiking the Oregon Trail."

Oregon Trail is Level 3 of the Triangle Defense.

The Triangle Defense, Level 3: Oregon Trail

THE GAME IS PLAYING YOUR KID

In addition to being a form of response cost, hiking the Oregon Trail can be thought of as a reward and a relief in some ways, much like Chill Time can be. For example, in the brain, dopamine levels off, adrenaline decreases, and melatonin resurges. In the home, the family talks and engages over shared activities in real time and then actually goes to sleep.

It's time to hike the Oregon Trail when Chill Time is not sufficient to curb your child's misbehavior or prevent it from recurring. For example, maybe your child breaks something, pretends to run away, hits you, or tells you to shut up (or worse) when you ask him to turn off the screen. These behaviors demonstrate that your child needs a break from the stimulation of the screen! So grant him one. Help him break that functional dependence on tech. Elevate to Level 3 by reminding your child that his behavior suggests he probably needs to take a relatively long break from screen time—one that far exceeds a mere two to five minutes. Let him know he's showing you that he needs to take a screen hiatus and hike the Oregon Trail. Keep in mind that you will find it effective to communicate this feedback gently and stoically, not with a big emotional reaction that, if he likes upsetting you, could inadvertently reward him for misbehaving.

Speaking of poise while communicating, notice that my former colleague's mother had already nixed the high school dance and that the father on the antidrug commercial had already denied permission to attend the unchaperoned party even in advance of the teens' provocative protests. When you consider the context of both cases, each parent was already at a Level 3 type of response following an earlier concern about conduct or safety, so even though the teens' shared protest of "I hate you!" was really harsh, the parents' letting the protest itself go made perfect sense and was all that was required.

Notice also that the parents' Level 3 type of response didn't limit electronics, per se, but social activities that would provide opportunities to behave in the same problematic ways the teens were already behaving at home. Similarly, in your home, hiking the Oregon Trail can simply mean taking a break from any stimulating activities that your child's current behavior doesn't warrant, including screen-based recreation but also parties, play dates, and sleepovers. Hiking the Oregon Trail means taking time to settle down and re-center by bonding over tech-free activities like baking, reading, drawing, doing puzzles, completing little home improvement projects, or even literal hiking. I learned about using the Oregon Trail as a response cost from a mentor who referred to it as Pioneer Days.

Step III will describe how to estimate how long the hike on the Oregon Trail needs to last, but a good rule of thumb is that the duration needs to mirror how problematic the behavior was. In general, if your child escalates past Chill Time but soon pulls it together, then his hike on the Oregon Trail need not be very long—maybe a few hours.

Once your child has settled down and has come to hear instruction, see modeling, and experience outcomes aligned in teaching him the same thing, he will have learned his lesson, so no further teaching will be accomplished by continuing to limit something he enjoys. Plus he will appreciate that your limit is rational and sensible, as opposed to emotional and arbitrary. Recall the whole purpose of unplugging is to reconnect, which Junior won't feel safe to do with you if you seem to impose limits rashly or unpredictably.

Keep in mind that your child might test the limits so much that she ends up with no screen time at all for a while. As a father recently expressed in my office, "I'm afraid that if I use this approach, my daughter will keep acting out and end up with no screen time at all." I exclaimed, "Good! Her behavior will probably be easier to manage if she's not using electronics as frequently."

I reminded this father to follow his Technology Stimulates and Actions Speak instincts. Next, we talked about the over/under. This father simply needed to let his daughter care more about her screen time than he did and allow her actions to show him how long of a break she needed from screen-based activities. Until she could refrain from acting out when she encountered a limit, it didn't make sense for her to be granted the privilege of screen use anyway. During the screen hiatus, the girl and her dad spent more time together engaging in one of their favorite tech-free activities: taking saxophone lessons.

Another father I recently counseled told me that his son went on a tech-free camping trip with his friends for a few days. Upon the boy's return, the parents noticed how relaxed, sociable, and calm he was. He had been able to settle down because the pace and demands of today's world, which are largely driven by technology, were temporarily alleviated for him.

More recently still, a junior high student described to me how his parents had simply unplugged his Xbox for a few days, pretending that the device had suffered an unfortunate accident. By the time they plugged the Xbox back in, he decided he didn't really need it so badly after all, because he had rediscovered his love of backyard sports. I don't condone his parents' misrepresentation that the Xbox had broken down; I would have advised them to tell him what behaviors had cost him use of it and which of his jobs he needed to fulfill in order to get back the privilege of using it. However, the point is that the parents helped the boy kick the screen habit by figuratively ushering him into an extended hike on the Oregon Trail and literally ushering him back outside.

Despite your best efforts, and perhaps even stemming from a situation that didn't involve you at all, your child might veer off the Oregon Trail and escalate to the point of doing something that's illegal, hard to contain, or really dangerous. That's when you know it's time for the Xbox to encounter the X-Men. Yes—like the superheroes.

X-Men

If your son holds a knife over his forearm and threatens to cut himself if you don't unlock his iPad, what will you do? Do you give him access and thereby reinforce that kind of escalation? Do you deny him access and risk him seriously injuring himself? To some parents, dangerous double binds like this will sound extreme and unlikely; to others, they will sound all too familiar. In these precarious situations where the stakes couldn't be higher, you need help.

X-Men is Level 4 of the Triangle Defense.

The Triangle Defense, Level 4: X-Men

Level 4 is not often necessary, but it's critical to know of its existence. Rest assured that, should you need it, you can get X-tra help from your own list of superheroes. Who ya gonna call? Let's brainstorm:

- Your partner
- Your neighbor
- Your therapist
- A teacher
- A clergyperson

- An extended family member
- The police
- The emergency room (ER)
- A residential treatment center

Just because things get crazy, that doesn't mean you have to. Instead, get superheroic assistance. Precisely whom you call will depend on what the specific problem is. For example, if your daughter continues skipping class to meet up with friends even when she's been hiking the Oregon Trail all week, you probably call a psychologist who specializes in working with teens and families. What you've tried so far (Levels 1–3) is sound and well intentioned but is not working for some reason. You need help from a professional to determine what that reason is. For example, there might be anxiety or depression influencing your daughter's behavior. Such conditions can thwart the learning process and render ineffective your otherwise viable parenting approaches.

Or if your twelve-year-old son keeps disregarding your rules and finding ways of sneaking screen time during the hour each afternoon that you can't be home with him, maybe you call the college kid down the street and ask him if he wants to make a few bucks every day by babysitting, which in this case means just coming over to ensure that your son is doing his homework instead of flipping on an electronic device. Another option would be to enroll your son in a monitored study hall that's held after school.

Or, to return to the earlier example that involves an imminent threat, imagine that your seventeen-year-old son says he'll slit his wrist if you don't let him use his iPad. You might otherwise have been perplexed, but now you know that Level 4 spells it out for you: you need help keeping your son safe, so that might require you to get him to the ER.

The reason for decisive action in this Level 4 situation is that, as director of your family's Department of Health and Safety, you must protect safety at all costs. What a sorry state of affairs it would be if every time your son disagreed with you, he only needed to threaten self-harm or suicide for you to change your mind. Instead, when a child threatens self-harm or suicide, there are three possible explanations, and each typically merits the same course of action.

1. He is serious about harming or killing himself and needs to be kept safe. By escorting your child to the ER, you have saved his body, life, or both. If he refuses to go with you and you're mightier than

he, you can follow the law of the animal kingdom—might makes right—and get him safely in the car. If he refuses and he's mightier than you, you'll need to overmatch his strength with your wisdom. Depending on where you live, you might call 911, the local police, or the Department of Mental Health (DMH) and tell them that your son is threatening self-harm and you can't get him to the ER. Dialing 911 should get an immediate response, but an ambulance can be costly. The police are a less expensive option, offering escort by way of police car, but police officers typically are not trained mental-health professionals like the Psychiatric Emergency Team (PET) from the DMH. However, the PET's response time can be lengthy.

2. He is making an idle threat. Threats like that need to be extinguished. How? X-Men is a response cost. You need to make it "expensive" for him to idly threaten self-harm. There are few places more boring for your child than the ER waiting room, where he will sit with nothing to do until he has to try to

convince the mental-health evaluator that he was upset enough to threaten suicide but not upset enough to mean it. At stake is a three-day stay in the hospital, which most patients would consider a form of basic punishment. Sitting in the ER waiting room cleanly combines Levels 1–4: the provocative statement didn't merit undue attention, resulted in lots of chill time and a screen hiatus, and reached a ceiling that communicated that such provocations result in decisive limits.

3. He is making an idle threat but then inadvertently hurts himself while trying to "prove" that he was serious. Feigned demonstrations of self-harm, whether they inadvertently result in injury, are behaviors that need to be extinguished. How? Same course of action: protect his safety by escorting him to the ER or arranging for transport there.

Implementing the Triangle Defense

Here's an example of how quickly a situation can escalate and a demonstration of how to set limits on a seemingly endless escalation by issuing the appropriate response costs. The example is carried out from the bottom to the very top of the Triangle Defense so you know how to use it in its entirety, if necessary.

You: "Champ! Five minutes until you need to turn off the Xbox for dinner." *(You deliver a "fair warning." Ideally, your son is already keeping track of his own time, as will be discussed in Step III. But even if he is, you're being extra helpful by giving him a heads-up.)*

Junior: No response. *(Notice that had Junior replied, "Sure, Mom!" and turned off the screen immediately, you might have rewarded the self-control with a bonus of additional screen time later, or at least some verbal praise for his going with the flow. But in this instance he didn't. He ignored you altogether. Let's see how that works out for Junior.)*

You, five minutes later: "Okay, bud! It's time for dinner! Please turn it off!" *(You deliver a clear instruction. You want him to learn from your words that dinner trumps Xbox. Plus, he can observe that you are near the dinner table yourself, so what he observes you doing is consistent with what he hears you saying. You might need to issue some response* costs to help him follow your instruction, but that's not clear yet.)

Junior: "Aww, no way! C'mon!" (He attempts to provoke you and to keep playing. It looks like you will, in fact, need to buttress your instruction and modeling with some response costs.)

You: "Make a good choice." (You accurately perceive his complaint to require no more than Level 1 of the Triangle Defense, so you simply Let It Go and do not respond to it directly. Rather, you modify your instruction in a way that implicitly reminds him of what's at stake—his access to the rewarding activity.)

Junior: "But Mom! You don't understand!" (He's ramping up. Here is the beginning of the Extinction Burst. Because you're holding the line, he's testing your commitment, so you must be doing it right.)

You: "Now you need to turn it off and chill for a minute before coming to the table." (You're moving up to Level 2 so that dinner can be pleasant.)

Junior: "Forget that!" (It's clear that Chill Time isn't going to do the trick because he's not agreeing to try chilling out.)

You: "Now it's off until tomorrow morning instead of going back on after dinner." *(You've just hopped on the Oregon Trail.)*

Junior: "What? You *suck!*" *(The Extinction Burst is still . . . bursting. You set a limit that clearly had an impact on him. Now he's trying to get you to back down, or at least provoke you into an escalation. He's going to need a longer hike on the Oregon Trail.)*

You: "Now it's off until tomorrow afternoon." *(You didn't reward or relieve his Burst; you held the line. He's the press and you're Phil Jackson. You even oriented Junior to how his Burst backfired for him in that it only extended the hike on the Oregon Trail. At this point, you can calmly turn off the Xbox.)*

Junior: "I can't believe this! I might as well kill myself!" *(He isn't getting it. He's either threatening you or seriously thinking this game is worth dying for. Either way, you know what to do: extinguish the threat and ensure his safety.)*

You: "Get in the car. We're going to the ER."

[Or alternatively, if you can't get him in the car safely:

You: "I'm calling 911 [or the local police, or the DMH]."]

Junior: "What the %&$ are you talking about?" *(Notice that if, at this point, instead of escalating further, Junior had backed down because he had been bluffing, you probably would have been able to issue some Chill Time, then eat dinner together, then ensure that he hiked the Oregon Trail for the next day or so, and you wouldn't have needed to get him to the ER. But in this example, Junior didn't back down. He continued to challenge you.)*

You: "If you're serious, I need to keep you safe. If you're threatening me, it doesn't get you Xbox. I'm not sure which it is, because we don't talk that way around here. I'll let the experts at the hospital decide." *(Perfect! Anarchy doesn't rule, and you recognize that you need extra help. By this time, you have also called in your partner or whomever. Notice also that you're calmly speaking to your son like the twentysomething he'll soon be by inviting him into your thought process.)*

Junior: "I'm not going anywhere! You'll have to drag me there!" *(You've reached the top of the Burst. You're gridlocked.)*

As previously described, if you're mightier, you can choose to get him into the car or call for X-Men. If he's mightier, you'll have to advance right to calling for X-Men. In either case, you made the right move; either he was serious and you just saved his life, or he was threatening you and it backfired on him.

It's important that you have Junior help you pay the expensive ER or ambulance bill so he doesn't get the idea that he can sock it to you for a few thousand dollars by threatening self-harm again. How do you have Junior help you pay the bill? Don't reinvent the wheel. Arrange it so that his response has come at a cost to him. Refer back to chapter 3's discussion of how to have him pay his phone bill. Essentially, you will reallocate monies you otherwise would have granted him willingly, have him work off his bill (setting additional response costs if he refuses), or both.

Once the proverbial iron is cool, you can talk more about what happened and provide further rationale for your decision and an orientation of what he can expect going forward. Something as simple as, "There's no room in our home for any device that would lead to you considering suicide or even talking to me that way. Once the ER bill is paid and I don't hear you talk that way for a few weeks, we can reconsider you having access to electronics again. But I need to be convinced you're not going to resort to threatening me or yourself again."

Using Level 4 of the Triangle Defense is not going to be pretty. You have committed to reining in your child's aggression and helping him channel it appropriately. That's no cakewalk. Psychologists Stephen Mitchell and Margaret Black (1995) analogize the toning down of adolescent aggression as follows: "One cannot put a wild bronco in harness and hope for a comfortable ride through Central Park."

It's practically impossible to set and enforce reasonable limits on an aggressive child when you're depleted. Recall HALT. Whatever it takes, within healthy reason, *you must take care of yourself*. Taking walks, yoga, prayer, massage, therapy, meditation, making love with your spouse, drinking herbal tea . . . we each "find our chi" in different ways, but the key is to *find* it. At a clinic where I once worked, an administrator said she found her chi nightly by doing a Sudoku puzzle in the bath while she sipped a glass of wine. Not my cup of tea (or glass of wine, as it were), but it worked for her. I tend to find inner balance by accessing my inner child. I "find center" atop a paddleboard.

And in the moments that most try my patience, I tap into my favorite permanent objects, like Phil

Jackson maintaining his composure with the pushy press. Or I grin as I remember Jeff Bridges in *The Big Lebowski* staying Zen while firmly asserting himself: "This aggression will not stand, man."

Consider some of the ways you stay composed. When you're depleted and it's hard to stay calm, how do you rejuvenate and restore? How do you take care of yourself? If you don't, how do you imagine you would like to? When was the last time your inner child came out to play?

It is critical that you pause to generate some responses to these questions before taking Step III. Once you identify viable options for getting the rest and perspective you need, you will be ready to tailor the solution to match your family's needs and values.

★ ★ ★

Now you know how to effectively teach your child in the same three ways that he naturally learns. You know how to talk to him and how to play good defense if he goes on the offensive. And you've developed expertise about your family's screen problem in a way that acknowledges its magnitude while keeping it in its proper context. As a result, the problem finally looks solvable and you not only feel like you could help Junior unplug, you also see some ways you might reconnect with him. In our game, we're way ahead, and it's clear that we're going to win. One step left.

STEP III:

Tailor the Solution to Fit Your Family's Needs and Values

Chapter 6

Measuring Your Family's Progress

*"A drunk man will find his way home, but
a drunk bird may get lost forever."*

—Shizuo Kakutani

N ow that you've become the expert on your family's screen problem and embraced a solution, let's take our final step. It's time to make your family's day-to-day life together look just the way you want it to, so that you can take a breath with time remaining to enjoy watching your child thrive and your family members get along. You need to know how to measure even abstract concepts that previously were too vague to be of much use to you when trying to problem-solve.

Operationalizing

Notice that all the abstract terms discussed so

far, from *privilege* to *punishment*, from *school performance* to *home behavior*, beg to be operationalized. That is, these abstract terms need working definitions. If you want your son to be more respectful or earn better grades before he can play longer, then you'll need to define and make measurable concepts like *better*, *longer*, and *more respectful* so everyone is on the same page about what's required and what's at stake. If you can pare down abstract concepts into two dimensions, you'll eventually figure out if and how they're working; if you stay in 3-D, where the possibilities are infinite, you're as lost as the drunken bird.

Dimension #1: Time

Keeping track of behaviors and their outcomes across time can intimidate parents, but it doesn't need to. Try imagining a simple timeline.

Let's discuss two key concepts that can be tracked along this horizontal x-axis of time: sequence and length. First, let's plot the order, or sequence, of the three jobs of being a kid. Then let's estimate duration, or length, that the response cost lasts when a job isn't done.

Sequence: Place the Horse in Front of the Cart

Recently a couple I was meeting with said their daughter was refusing to do homework despite their best efforts to encourage and support her. She had offered them a deal, and they were inclined to accept it: Their daughter would agree to do that night's homework if the family first went to the restaurant of her choice for dinner. The parents were thrilled that their daughter sounded so willing to do her homework, and all it would cost them was a dinner out, which they would all enjoy anyway. It sounded to them like a win-win.

I cautioned them that while the proposal sounded great, their daughter would likely enjoy the dinner, then "inexplicably" encounter obstacles to completing her homework, like hearing that all her friends were simultaneously online for one night only and were desperately awaiting her virtual presence. The couple looked like they didn't believe me until I reminded them that they didn't get paid before going to work, but after. Their daughter had craftily suggested the bribe precisely because it would allow her to get her proverbial dessert—or in this case dinner—first, and at the restaurant of her choice!

The parents needed to tap into their Actions Speak instinct. A deal that had a better chance of working out for both parties would be one in which the reward of dinner was earned not by way of a verbal promise to do the homework, but by way of the action of finishing it.

Such a deal would grant the girl her wish but would grant the parents theirs too. The deal would reward task completion instead of procrastination. It would leave the girl feeling satisfied emotionally, then physically. It would leave the parents feeling proud and would lift any dinnertime apprehension about how their daughter would do on the homework because she would have already done it.

Does that kind of a deal sound too good to be true? It doesn't need to. It's realistic. In the working world, the responsibility or behavior precedes the privilege or reward, which is why my reminder to the parents caught their attention: you go to work *before* you get paid. The ideal deal simply keeps the horse where it belongs: in front of the cart. The jobs of school and home have to precede the job of having fun.

Anticipate Crafty Appeals

Parents who have a conceptual understanding of how to sequence responsibilities and privileges can still become trapped by too quickly accepting crafty appeals proposed by their children. These are appeals that *sound* really good, but they obscure the fact that the cart would lead the horse. Here are three such appeals, which you should not accept without careful review.

Crafty Appeal #1: "Let me buy on credit"

Remember George Wendt's character Norm on *Cheers*? He sat at the bar ordering beer after beer, but you never saw him pay. On one classic episode, Ted Danson, playing bartender Sam Malone, produced Norm's storied tab from behind the bar: a three-ring binder full of receipts! Norm had been buying on credit for years. When finally presented with the tab, Norm owed his drink total plus *a lot* of interest. The tab was the response cost that followed the rewards.

If your child wants to buy something on credit, you don't have to automatically accept the deal. You're not Sam Malone, you're an exec for FICO and your job is to assign credit scores! Whether you accept the deal depends on her credit score, which you get to adjust based on her history.

Is her credit low, like that of the girl who offered her parents the "dessert-first" appeal? She needs to build up more of a credit history before you issue her a card with a decent credit limit. "Sorry, sweetie. We're going to dinner at the restaurant of your choice only *after* your homework is done." Or, "Sorry, hon. We're not watching TV this morning before school. When you consistently get to school on time, then we can try that."

Is her credit high? You consider allowing her to buy on credit and discuss the terms of the transaction, including the interest rate (response cost). "Sure—you're really reliable about finishing your assignments, so you can go to the matinee with your friend and then come home to finish your report. But that means you really have to finish it, even if you have to stay up late despite being tired. When you do so, then you'll be showing me you can probably be trusted to do something fun before you finish your homework again next weekend."

In my office the other day, a boy with a low credit score appealed to his mother and she nearly accepted, stating to her son, "Okay, but if we give you privileges, you have to self-regulate." Mom was on the right track, but the sequence needed to be reversed and the phrasing could have been more motivating to him. A more effective narration would have been, "When you self-regulate, then you earn privileges."

Crafty Appeal #2: "I need a break after school"
Your child asks for screen time as an "after-school snack." Your child has a point: school can be considered the horse, and screen time the cart. He has attended school and wants some screen time. That's legitimate. I'm a huge fan of kids getting a break after school, *before* beginning homework; this one might actually work, even though it places the privilege of screen time before the responsibility of homework and obscures the typical response cost that there's no screen reward if the work isn't done.

The key is to put parameters on the break, ensuring the cart stays attached to the horse so the result isn't a response cost in the form of plummeting grades. Merely attending school doesn't merit four uninterrupted hours of screen time. Instead, grant a bit of screen time, like a half hour, that's followed by another horse-cart pairing: homework, then something else enjoyable. Remember to try to both unplug and reconnect. Maybe the ultimate reward is screen time, but ideally it's a tech-free activity with you, like a one-on-one game of basketball in the driveway. At a minimum, try to connect. Maybe the ultimate reward is an hour of screen time that's at least shared with you or another family member.

Notice that you could also help Junior draft a rider that takes account of the day's events as well as those occurring the day prior. Completing yesterday's homework in advance of bedtime nets Junior an after-school break of thirty minutes before beginning today's homework. As long as he finishes today's homework before bedtime, he gets to delay the start of tomorrow's homework by thirty minutes, and so on. Should he struggle to finish today's homework, then it makes sense to help him get started earlier tomorrow, instead of allowing him to first take a break. As long as you're not painfully annoying about doing so, your helping him get started earlier will not be a basic punishment, but a response cost.

Crafty Appeal #3: "Short screen breaks will help me complete my work"

Many students feel like they have so much to do that they force themselves to sit down for thirty or sixty minutes and try to work the entire time. Typically, they become distracted after just a few minutes and spend most of the session trying to get back on track. They understandably complain, then, about the double bind in which they find themselves: If they delay, the homework only piles up. If they try to have a marathon homework session, they fatigue quickly.

To help your daughter move things along without tiring out, you might try arranging a miniature horse-cart paradigm, in which she studies for nine minutes, then immediately takes a one-minute break. One minute is not enough time to start a video game or get sucked into a TV show. It's just enough time for her to stretch or get a drink or check in with you to update you on her progress and see what you're making for dinner, and then hop back into it. And it's only nine minutes until the next break, so hopping back into the work isn't as hard.

After sixty minutes, your child will have only taken six minutes "off," which she will have spent rejuvenating so she will not have worn herself out! Most exciting to your child, this kind of approach taps into her Two Marshmallows instinct, as it ends up ultimately netting her more uninterrupted screen time at the end of the day than she would have had trying to grab bits of it here and there while chipping away at her work. She'll stay on track, finish the work sooner, and enjoy having more time left over than usual. And by having gone without (the recreational use of) screens while completing her homework, she might ultimately decide that they aren't really what appeal to her when it comes time to spend the precious free time she's worked hard to earn.

Length: Estimate the Time Required to Hike the Oregon Trail

Recall that the Triangle Defense is your guide to issuing response costs. Level 1 of the Triangle Defense does not specify how long you need to Let It Go, because you simply do so until the irritating behavior extinguishes. Level 2 of the Triangle Defense, Chill Time, entails issuing time-outs that last a minimum of two minutes and that gradually increase up to a maximum of about five minutes. So determining how long you implement either of the first two levels of the Triangle Defense is very straightforward. Determining the length that you'll need to issue Level 3, Oregon Trail, requires further explanation, which follows, and determining how long you need the help of X-Men is case by case; it depends on how much help you need to keep your kid healthy and safe, and yourself healthy and sane.

When it comes to estimating how long it will take Junior to hike the Oregon Trail, start with a working knowledge of how days can be chunked into three eight-hour periods: morning, afternoon, and evening. Plan a hike that takes Junior the rest of whatever period of the day you're in, then if necessary, extend the hike to stretch across the next period, repeating as necessary. For example, let's define *afternoon* as occurring between noon and 8:00 PM. Imagine it's 4:00 PM, and Junior pitches a fit when you tell him it's time to turn off the video game to leave for baseball practice. You largely ignore his fit in recognition of the fact that the car ride to baseball will serve as natural Chill Time for him. Give him a few minutes of that ride where he's not reinforced with your attention or with any escalation and things are quiet and calm.

But let's say Junior carries the fit into the car and it lasts for more than a few minutes. You astutely observe that the situation has climbed past Chill Time and merits a Level 3 response. So you gently tell Junior that he needs to hike the Oregon Trail for the rest of the afternoon (until 8:00, when you mark the onset of evening, the next chunk of the day). Between baseball practice and 8:00 PM, if he has faithfully hiked the Oregon Trail by having discontinued his fit, participated in baseball practice, returned home without begging for the screen, willingly eaten dinner, and engaged with the family, then he has effectively completed the hike.

However, if Junior "veers off" the Oregon Trail between baseball practice and 8:00 PM, then progressively revise your estimate to include the next eight-hour chunk of the day. For example, if he gets back in the car after practice and gives you attitude, tell him that he is taking longer to hike the Oregon Trail than you had hoped and that you now anticipate he'll be hiking it until at least the next morning. Then he will either keep pushing you, incorrectly thinking that you'll revise your estimate downward, or he will start to grasp that his actions are dictating how long the hike is going to last. Once he grasps the concept and behaves appropriately through the end of the eight-hour period you've most recently stipulated, the hike is over.

The savvy reader will calculate that chunking the day in the fashion described above would define *morning* as beginning at 4:00 AM. You might say, "Wait a minute. Allowing my child to turn on electronics at that hour would be implicitly encouraging him to go spelunking." I agree.

When your child earns access to an electronic and that access is set to begin the next morning, you have three viable options. First, you can modify the chunks of the day to fit your routine. The chunks don't have to be uniform. For example, maybe evening runs from 8:00 PM to 8:00 AM. If you choose to adjust the timing, make sure to be clear about it and jot it down so that the whole family can follow the definitions with consistency. When kids feel like you're being clear and consistent, there's less potential for them to bend the rules or become resentful of the rules changing arbitrarily.

Second, you could go ahead and use 4:00 AM as the marker that morning has begun, but not as the first moment that screen time becomes available. In your home, maybe earning electronics access that's set to begin the following "morning" effectively means access is set to begin the following afternoon upon returning from school (unless there's no school or important commitments the following day).

Third, you could allow your child to wake up at 4:00 AM or anytime thereafter and play if he wants to. If he abuses the latitude he's granted in this regard, you'll know it by virtue of his actions: he will become irritable or act out soon thereafter. In doing so, he will have earned less or no screen time to subsequently cash in, because his rider already specifies that screen time is contingent upon his home behavior. Or perhaps he won't abuse the latitude, but he'll get really tired later in the day and go to bed earlier that night. In either case, getting up so early will come with response costs, whether you help issue those or whether they occur naturally. Or maybe he'll handle the latitude just fine and learn that sometimes it's fun to get up early to do something you enjoy as long as you keep yourself "together" the rest of the day.

Additional Crafty Appeals

A few pages ago, we discussed three crafty appeals that, if accepted, would place the cart before the horse. There also exist three legitimate-sounding appeals that your child might make that threaten to truncate the Oregon Trail with a dead end.

Crafty Appeal #4: "I need the computer and the Internet for school"

Expect that while he hikes the Oregon Trail, Junior will correctly point out that his homework assignment requires the use of a computer and/or the Internet. If you grant him the use, he will probably wander back to games or nonacademic websites. So what do you do?

As the psychologist who taught me Family Systems would say, "The symptom can never be the answer!" In other words, the intricacy of the problem can never trump the ingenuity of the person. In response to this crafty appeal, you'll need to unplug and reconnect. Get creative and help facilitate the assignment's completion, but in a way that upholds your limits on Junior's technology use.

You have several options of how to do so, depending on the teacher's requirements. For example, if Junior conveniently "needs" the Internet to conduct "research," then accompany him to the library, where he can find plenty of sources for his report. Or if retrieving a source online or getting onto a computer (perhaps one that's even school issued) is "part of the assignment," then you can supervise Junior as he completes the task, ensuring that he does nothing else. As he completes the task, reinforce him. If he refuses to complete it, issue response costs according to the Triangle Defense.

Or if Junior conveniently "has to" type his report, you might restrict electronics but arrange old-school accommodations to facilitate completion of the assignment. I know of an amazing product that allows you to type without even accessing the Internet. It's the coolest thing. It's called a typewriter. My great-great-grandfather George Jewett was one of the early developers of the typewriter. He presented his Jewett Typewriter in 1901 at the World's Fair in Paris, to great success. Tell Junior you bought him a vintage Jewett Typewriter because you want him to join the hipster writers and choose typewriters over computers because they come fully loaded with . . . nothing. There are no apps and no Internet, so there are no inherent distractions. The author just writes.

Or savvy Junior might claim that he is "required" to submit some assignments online, perhaps by way of a program like Google Docs. That might be true, but don't let your child con you into a bad decision under the guise of getting homework done. Your young poker opponent is bluffing again: Junior *himself* doesn't have to get online to submit his homework. You can make the submission for him, perhaps by scanning the work and sending it in. Or you might explain to the teacher what's going on at home and request that Junior temporarily be allowed to manually hand in his assignments.

Crafty Appeal #5: "I need a phone for emergencies"

On the heels of Junior's appeal that his homework assignment requires computer or Internet access will come the argument that he needs his smartphone "in case of an emergency." This is another appeal that threatens to prematurely end his hike on the Oregon Trail.

Help him stay on it by reading him an altered

version of his Miranda rights: "You're correct: you have the right to a phone. Sometimes we do need to reach you immediately and vice versa. If you can't afford a cool phone by getting a job or by behaving enough for me to reward you with one, we'll provide you with the simplest phone on earth. It'll call one number: mine." You can find these phones online, or you can use an app like Ignore No More to limit the functionality of the phone Junior already possesses.

Crafty Appeal #6: "This was a gift, so it's mine"

Another appeal Junior will make is that you (or someone else) gifted him the game or device, or that he purchased it with his own money, and thus he owns it. In one of the *Diary of a Wimpy Kid* books, the narrator debates simply not asking for a "normal" gift like a video game or toy one year: "What I've realized is that every time you get something cool for your birthday or for Christmas, within a week it's being used against you."

Many parents are careful about limiting something they've previously endorsed. They recognize that they are sending a mixed message if they buy a gift and then ask that it not be used. Indeed, giving electronic gifts without any agreement about how they are to be used can quickly backslide into situations ripe for mutual resentment. Kids start to resent their parents for giving a gift that seems to still belong to their parents; parents start to resent their kids because they've given the kids a gift that is seemingly being abused.

If this topic is a concern of yours, it's probably because you have already given the gift, so it's too late to arrange terms and conditions now. Next time, do so up front, like Apple does for you by supplying that enormous document when you download the latest software update. For now, recall Phil Jackson's quote. Your wisdom has to overmatch your child's strength, so maybe you choose to transcend the ownership debate entirely, as alluded to in chapter 3.

Junior strongly asserts that he owns the Xbox, so you wisely and calmly remind him that you pay for the wall, the outlet, the electricity, the TV, and the Internet. Gently orient him to the fact that, if necessary for his own health or safety, you'll need to flip the circuit breaker for his room, password-protect the router or device, or carry the power cord with you to the office. Then remind him that he can choose, by way of his behavior, how quickly he regains access to these things: if he fulfills the first two jobs of being a kid, you will help him enjoy the third. You stay connected with him as you help him to unplug. Until he regains access to the power, password, or accessories necessary for the gifted console to work, he maintains possession of a nonfunctional device.

In essence, what's required in gift situations is a shared understanding of the difference between *the gift* (the device) and the *use* of the gift (the playing of the device). Your teen might be "ready for a phone," meaning he is fully capable of appropriately managing his own phone all day and evening, but he might need some help turning it off so he's not texting with friends all night.

★ ★ ★

Now you know how to plot abstract concepts along the horizontal line of time, including being able to sequence responsibilities and privileges and determine the length of the Oregon Trail. Now you need to know how to measure the degree of responsibility and privilege.

Dimension #2: Degree

You can measure the amount or volume of something by rating it along the vertical line of degree. Our kids measure the degree of abstract concepts, such as popularity, by way of "Likes." It's important that the adults have a way to measure the degree of abstract concepts, like responsibility and privilege, too.

To do so, let's keep the horse and the cart along the horizontal line of time. Responsibilities like homework and privileges like screen time stay on the x-axis, so we'll measure their degree up the y-axis, like this:

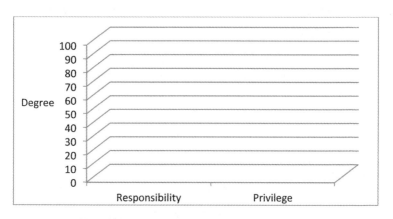

Responsibility and Privilege in Terms of Degree

Where to Set the Bar

As I mentioned earlier, you want to award a degree of privilege that rivals the degree of responsibility your child demonstrates. The return should be worth his investment.

Let's say Junior is fifteen years old. He's attending school and doing homework, but his grades are Cs and he's calling his mother nasty names when he doesn't get what he wants. Overall he's bargaining hard for fun, but he's barely completing only one of his two tougher jobs: school. The job of home, particularly minding his parents, needs plenty of work. On the whole, Junior demonstrates a relatively low degree of responsibility. For simplicity, you might rate the degree of his responsibility in terms of a percentage or letter grade. Call it 30 percent, which is an F. He gets some minimal credit for attending school and doing homework, but in terms of developing into a respectful man who's performing to his potential, he's got a ways to go!

So here's what you do with the 30 percent responsibility: you also rate 30 percent privilege. Your graph would look like this:

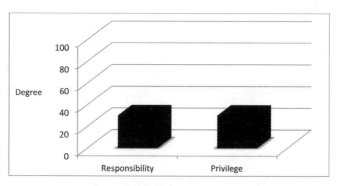

Low Responsibility – Low Privilege

Now decide what an F level of privilege would realistically entail. For example, tell him he has earned the privilege of having you pay for his tutoring so that he can get those Cs up to at least Bs. When he says he expects a higher degree of privilege, like a smartphone, gently tell him no, and explain that you can't see a reason to finance the opportunity for him to speak as disrespectfully to his female peers as he does to his mother. Instead of buying him a smartphone because he expects or bargains for one, invite him to draft a rider that gets him thinking about the responsibilities that would merit the level of privilege he's requesting. If he needs a visual aid, show him what his bar graph looks like now and what it would need to look like in order for him to earn a smartphone.

Junior won't find the present degree of privilege satisfactory, and that's good. You want him to strive for more. Let's say Junior does so. He gets the point and improves his grades to As and Bs and you regularly hear him speaking respectfully to his mother. Then it makes sense to help him continue learning how to talk to girls besides his mother, because he'll need plenty of practice at it. So you're ready to help him finance that smartphone. You could rate his degree of responsibility at a decent level—call it 70 percent.

So the degree of privilege should be rated at about 70 percent as well. Your graph would look like this:

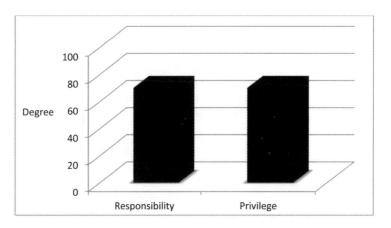

Adequate Responsibility – Adequate Privilege

In this situation, you might offer to pay for 70 percent of the smartphone or 70 percent of the conceivable text messages and minutes he uses each month.

The best-case scenario would be that Junior is making As or otherwise demonstrating that he is putting forth his very best academic effort. He's speaking respectfully to both parents, socializing, and even participating in extracurricular activities. His degree of responsibility is high, so the degree of privilege can be high too. Maybe you pay for an entire phone or unlimited, A-plus-level (100 percent) text messaging and minutes on his plan, which could be depicted like this:

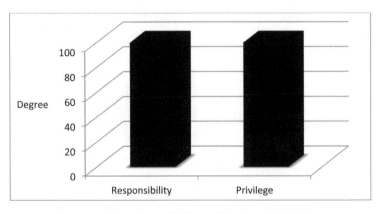

Optimal Responsibility – Optimal Privilege

This ideal scenario really captures the essence of the successful college experience: when you get your stuff done, then you can do whatever you want. College can be misconstrued as the one adult opportunity to play before you work—if you work at all. But that misconception won't allow you to stay in college very long. Similar to inviting Junior to draft a rider, try selling him on the idea that the true essence of college can begin right now and that the degree of responsibility he demonstrates will speak to the degree of electronics privilege he's ready for. Easy sell.

After all, he doesn't need to wait until he's

eighteen and living in a dorm to watch Netflix before he goes to bed. Rather, he can practice balancing this privilege with his responsibilities as soon as you're convinced he's ready for it. How can he convince you? Probably by behaving in ways that suggest he's getting enough sleep, like waking up on time, staying active, and speaking respectfully throughout the day.

Before we continue, let's stay with this best-case scenario for a moment. Let's lay to rest any debate about whether it's fair to use grades to rate how responsibly Junior is fulfilling the job of school. Such a debate is sort of another red herring. Of course grades reflect academic performance! However, Junior has a point if he argues that grades may not reliably reflect academic *effort*. So I would suggest rating the job of school based not *only* on grades, but on other measurable indicators of effort as well, including standardized test scores; parent, teacher, and tutor feedback; attendance at school and study sessions; and so forth.

Within your home, you can decide the degree of academic effort you require Junior to demonstrate in order to receive the degree of privilege he requests. For example, let's say Junior earns straight Bs but requests a smartphone plan that includes unlimited (A-plus-level) talk minutes and texts. You have to decide if you're okay with that arrangement. If you're not sure how to decide whether you're okay with it, ask yourself the following questions:

- Would performing at a B level—between 80 and 89 percent—at my job earn me unlimited—100 percent—praise from my boss and/or my customers and clients?

- Did performing at a B level get me into this job in the first place?

- Am I satisfied in my job? With its income? With the lifestyle it provides?

If you answered yes to most of these questions, then maybe Bs in exchange for unlimited talk and text is a fine arrangement for Junior. Once again, what's good for the gander might prove good for the goose.

If you answered no to most of the questions, then don't misrepresent the reality of your experience by letting Junior access unlimited screen time in exchange for Bs. Instead, rate a B level of privilege and pay for 80 to 89 percent of conceivable talk time and text messaging on his plan.

Additionally, if you are not satisfied in your job, you will want to stay mindful of how much you explicitly and implicitly communicate this fact to Junior. He won't be as motivated to perform if you've conveyed that enjoyment of one's ultimate career is not a permanent object. He'll conclude that all the striving you're asking him to do isn't worth it in the long run.

From Bobo to BOB

You are closer than ever to solving your family's screen problem and keeping your family connected instead of plugged in. As a busy parent, you now need easy ways to preside over your increasingly clean fishbowl.

Remember the family in which the son asked that his parents tap on his headset to get his attention? They declined his request. They recently returned to my office for a follow-up visit and proudly reported that their son was turning off the Xbox at the agreed-upon time without their having to ask him to do so, and thus their arguments had become extinct. How'd they do that?

They took five specific actions. First, the parents asked themselves the Bobo question and limited their son's exposure to violent games by refusing to rent or buy any new ones for him. Second, they were mindful of the over/under. They recognized that when they had to beg and plead for their son to turn off the Xbox and he simply continued to refuse, they were over-functioning and he was under-functioning. They were caring more than he did, and they decided not to do that anymore.

Third, they instead began to set measurable limits by sequencing responsibility ahead of privilege: no Xbox until he'd finished homework.

Fourth, they recognized a crafty appeal from their son to let him "buy on credit," and they accepted it only after mutually agreeing to a steep response cost—a 100 percent interest rate for exceeding the earned amount of screen time: for every extra minute their son played today, he spent two of the next day's minutes.

These four actions helped improve their situation dramatically. However, sometimes their son simply exceeded the earned amount of screen time while skipping dinner and paid the interest the following day, as agreed. His parents tried Dodging Friendly Fire by enjoying dinner by themselves, but they were discouraged at his skipping meals with them. So they tried unplugging the TV when the earned screen time was up, but doing so resulted in considerable tension among them, which usually brought the mood at dinner down anyway. They needed to get themselves out from between their son and his Xbox, while somehow getting their son to turn off the system at an appropriate time.

At my encouragement, they took one more action. They purchased a device online called BOB, which attaches to the TV and keeps track of screen time. By way of a secure computer program, BOB allows parents to award screen time as the child earns it. When the allotted time has been met, BOB turns off the TV. It's that simple. This particular family's son quickly found it useless to try to reason with BOB, so there was no more tension, even when time was up.

Cheaper options than BOB that sometimes do the trick include a kitchen timer or, if you already own a smartphone, the standard countdown feature. Although these methods still require you to be "the messenger," sometimes just the use of an objective time standard is sufficient for curbing whiny negotiations. Your child knows you're not miscalculating the end of screen time. Instead, the established time limit is entered into the timer, which does the rest. I use my iPhone's timer feature frequently to orient my daughter to the passage of an agreed-upon amount of screen time. When it dings, she rarely pushes for "just one more minute," because like the teen whose parents used BOB, she knows that a machine was objectively tracking the agreed-upon amount of time.

When you need to monitor the nature of the content on a device, not just the length of time for which that device is used, look to additional methods. Sites like opendns.org offer products and services that compile the browser history (before Junior clears the cache) and enable you to filter Internet content across devices. For more specific app tracking, I recommend using Mac App Blocker or Windows Application Blocker, which allow you to designate what apps your child is able to access and at what times of day.

Or you can set yourself as the administrator on your child's devices and designate him as a user. This works particularly well in conjunction with sharing an iTunes and iCloud address with one another so that you can see what games he's playing and sites he's visiting. He can see which sites you're visiting, too, which is a great way to model for him how to stay away from inappropriate ones. You are doing so, aren't you?

Or you might get really fancy and pay to consult with the geeks behind the Genius Bar or the geniuses on the Geek Squad. They'll supply you with cool ideas too. To procure yet additional ideas on how to track your child's online activity, use technology responsibly to prevent Junior's misuse of technology by conducting a simple Internet search. There are lots of other tracking practices and products out there to choose from.

Notice that relying upon these supports makes things easier on you, as if you're calling in some mild-mannered X-Men to preemptively take the load off. Good for you. You're busy and can't be expected to monitor your household without a little support from time to time. Use the energy you save to take care of yourself or invite your family into some recreational activities. The job of having fun is not reserved just for kids! While endeavoring to reconnect with your kids, don't forget to reconnect with your inner kid. Whether alone or with your family:

- When was the last time you went on a bike ride?

- Have you ever been to your city's library just to browse?

- How long has it been since you've checked if you can see any stars where you live?

The Kill Switch

You might already be anticipating that implementing these monitoring methods can backfire. Kids often know more about circumventing supervisory aids than parents know about setting them up. Parents then feel stuck, because there appears to be no way to keep tabs. The Reverse Hierarchy is clearly at play, and your once-civilized life begins to resemble the animal kingdom where might makes right . . . and the kids seem to have all the might. You do everything this book recommends, and your kid laughs in your face and sneaks an electronic device right out from under you.

Even if the scene in your home regresses to such a state—even if all else fails—there is hope. Recall from this book's opening pages the idea that *any* electronics use *at all* is itself a privilege.

If the law of the animal kingdom threatens, you're still king of the jungle. You're stronger than your kid, your wisdom overmatches his strength, or both. In any case, you can impose order by temporarily unplugging altogether: no screens at all—maybe even no electricity at all—until your kid demonstrates respect for household rules of even more basic kinds. I see a family in therapy who refers to this response cost as "throwing the kill switch." The parents explained to their kids that such a Draconian response cost would only be issued if the children's behavior became so primitive as to require it.

Once you throw it, the kill switch might have to remain tripped for quite some time. Don't panic. It's a good problem you're solving here.

Pretend you've gone camping. You'll survive. You'll probably grow closer with one another as you hold hands and stumble around in the dark. Let the inconvenience be a bigger deal to your kid than to you and he will get motivated to turn things around. I realize this scenario might cause Junior's grades to take a hit. You have to decide how far you want to take it. That's part of tailoring the solution to fit your family's needs and values. You might decide throwing the kill switch on all electronics is worth it because while graduating with good grades is important, it's not as important as graduating without having become a total jerk.

As your child begins to fulfill his jobs again, you accurately rate a low degree of responsibility and accordingly reinstate a low degree of electronics privilege. If he starts to abuse the privilege, you might have to throw the kill switch again. Alternatively, if he fulfills increasingly more of his jobs, then reinstate more electronics use, and so on. Ultimately the hierarchy will return to its upright position, and structured freedom will reign again.

When the Ideal Hierarchy is in effect and your kid is beginning to self-monitor his electronics use, then what? Do you have to stay so vigilant, or might you actually be able to back off and watch your kid balance his jobs? How relaxing and satisfying does that scenario sound? It's coming.

Chapter 7

Scaffolding: When to Back Off

"If a building looks better under construction than it does when finished, then it's a failure."
—Douglas Coupland

Rearing children is like constructing skyscrapers. The parent is the scaffolding and the child is the building. The scaffolding surrounds and projects just higher than the building . . . the building catches up with it . . . the scaffolding then raises the bar. The scaffolding is distinct from the building, but it stands alongside the building to offer guidance and support, ensuring that the building stays straight as it grows. Ultimately the building stands on its own and the scaffolding is gradually deconstructed, from the top down.

Setting Your Level of Monitoring

Think of your scaffolding as representing a third bar in the *x-y* coordinate bar graph of time and degree. The scaffolding bar shows how much monitoring you need to provide, so it goes in the opposite direction as the other two. What your child might be asking for is to demonstrate a minimal degree of responsibility *after* enjoying a premium degree of privilege, with you out of his way (or not monitoring him at all), like this:

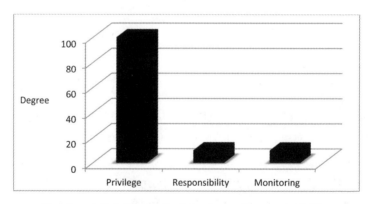

Optimal Privilege before Low Responsibility, with Low Monitoring

This is just another way of depicting the Reverse Hierarchy. Notice the reversal of the first two bars and how out of proportion they are: high privilege in front of low responsibility. You'll know your child has succeeded in bringing about this state of affairs if you are left bribing him to complete basic tasks by virtue of reminding him that he's already enjoying various luxuries. If this is the case, what you have to do for a while is provide extra monitoring to oversee and ensure that his responsibilities precede his privileges, and that both of those start small and move up incrementally, like in the kill switch scenario or the Justin Bieber rider example, where Biebs is offered water in exchange for showing up on time. The paradigm you need to construct can be depicted like this:

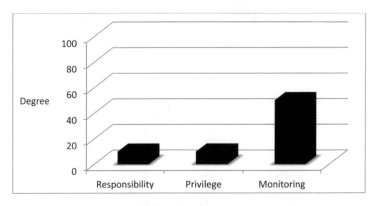

**Low Responsibility before Low Privilege,
with Adequate Monitoring**

As your child's degree of responsibility increases, so too does his degree of privilege, and thus the degree of monitoring decreases. Maybe you get feedback from the teacher that his academic effort has improved, so you increase his screen time and begin checking his grades weekly instead of daily. Remember that at the very end of the project, you want the building to stand on its own:

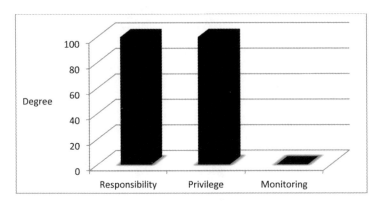

Optimal Responsibility before Optimal Privilege, with Low or No Monitoring

Let's practice measuring the relative degrees of responsibility, privilege, and monitoring across time. Consider the following two examples, each representing opposite ends of the continuum of possibilities.

In this first example, your son displays a lot of responsibility in advance of enjoying a commensurate degree of privilege. You use opendns.org, and from what you can tell, your son's Internet history is clean. You have observed that he treats women, including his mother and his girlfriend, with respect. There's no evidence to suggest that he is interacting inappropriately or unsafely with friends, whether in person or virtually. Together, you use Mac App Blocker or BOB here and there to help him stay on track, but he doesn't complain about your oversight and he typically wraps everything up before a decent bedtime. And if he stays up a little later than you suggest or model, he still gets up on time the next day and gets to school on time, and he does all of it without getting cranky and disrespectful.

If this is the scenario at your house, then great job! In turn, you're proud of your son, so you not only offer the relief of providing minimal scaffolding, you offer rewards for his wise decisions and self-control, perhaps by paying for his Internet access and his phone service. Each household is unique in terms of what the parents can and will pay for or allow when it comes to electronics. In our example here, the general idea is to help your son gain access to a degree of privilege that rivals how responsibly he's behaving, just like he'll be able to do soon when he's out of the house.

Sure, you'll still want to trust your gut and stay attuned to your instincts, but you can turn their volume down a bit and relax a little. Plus, he sounds like a kid who you enjoy being around. So instead of hopping on your own electronic device because Junior's turning out so well, now would be a great developmental phase during which to connect with him at a deeper level before he does leave the house. Might it be a good time to take saxophone lessons together, like the father-daughter pair I described earlier? How about dueling banjos? Dueling Rubik's Cubes? Maybe it's time to get a pair or family pack of season tickets to the ballpark. Maybe you just spend time inventing something cool together like the families you watch on *Shark Tank*.

In the second example, your son's Internet history is constantly full of pornographic sites and he seems to objectify women in his interactions and relationships with them. You're having no fun asking yourself the Bobo Question because you definitely don't want him acting like what he's watching. Your instincts scream to you that he's not yet ready for any further Internet access or texting without more of your supervision. He's putting garbage into his brain and in turn treating others like garbage.

You have to temporarily work very hard, carefully choosing each word, explicitly instructing and demonstrably modeling healthy interactions for him as he struggles to "get it." In the meantime, you find that you often need to heavily supervise his activities, relying upon the higher levels of the Triangle Defense in order to issue expensive response costs for his inappropriate use of technology. You implement extra scaffolding in the form of help from your human and technological X-Men. And all along, you connect with him over any healthy pursuits you can find in common. Those pursuits might be pretty limited, but now is not the time to forego them and risk disconnecting from your son any further. Invite him to do something you can both tolerate doing together, like going to see an appropriate movie or tracking down the best burger in town.

As your son begins to use the Internet appropriately, you take down the highest level of the scaffolding. You continue to take the time to truly connect with him in what you do together, but you offer a little more space in terms of your monitoring, and you reward the more appropriate decisions you see him making by granting access to off-screen privileges he enjoys. When his browser history is cleaner still, you take down some more scaffolding and gradually extend the time he can use the Internet unsupervised. Your fishbowl is getting cleaner.

Getting Out of the Way

A few years ago, I met with an adolescent in family therapy. He was a junior at one of the most prestigious high schools in California. He also played a video game considered one of the most addictive on the market. The boy's father was an accomplished attorney. In a session I had with the two of them, the father complained that his son was playing the video game almost all night.

The boy protested, saying that he didn't stay up "that late" playing the game. His father countered that he was worried his son's grades were slipping as a function of playing the game late into the night. The boy exclaimed, "But Dad, I'm getting straight As!" I looked inquisitively at his father, who nodded that his son's report was accurate. The father paused pensively, then complained, "Well, you have to be in an extracurricular club or something."

Incredulous, the boy reminded his father that he had founded the fencing club. His father nodded again. The father looked defeated and searched for another concern. Upon finding it, he implored, "Well, you have to spend some time with friends or something." The boy smiled and replied, "C'mon, Dad. You were complaining all weekend that I was out with my friends."

The father looked at me for help, expecting me to agree that there must be some reason that his son shouldn't play the game so late into the evening. I had to help the father tap into his instincts and realize they'd already completed their mission: he'd reared a son whose activities were balanced. I gently said to the father something like, "I think your son is ready for college, where he can stay up as late as he wants. Where he's likely to continue thriving academically, socially, and in extracurriculars."

That was our last session. They didn't need me anymore, and the boy no longer needed much of his father's scaffolding. The boy had demonstrated enough responsibility to merit a collegiate degree of privilege, and he was only a junior in high school. He had figured out how to balance the three jobs of being a kid and was feasting on proverbial marshmallows. In short, he'd figured out how to work hard to play hard. Sure, he could have gotten a bona fide job too, but he also wasn't asking for his parents to underwrite a disproportionate or expensive degree of privilege. For the time being, he just wanted Dad to let him stay up late. A rider cannot and should not include every conceivable responsibility or privilege, anyway, for the simple reason that not everything in the adult world is arranged according to the Tree.

The preceding example is an illustration of how you want your general family situation to look by the time your kid leaves the house: you guide and monitor a little, he thrives and self-regulates a lot. To finish Step III, let's get an even clearer picture of how you want life to look in your home and for your child, and take immediate action to make that picture become manifest.

Chapter 8

Eye on the Prize

"I don't feel good all the time,
but all the time, I know it's all good."
—My former patient, age eighteen

My former patient's quip was profound, and we both knew it right away. Through two years of psychotherapy, she had come to apprehend the difference between happiness and contentment, and she understood how the former comes and goes while the latter endures. She had come to grasp the major life truth that she could be the final arbiter of her mood instead of the circumstance du jour. In so doing, she had won a battle with major depression. The snarky sixteen-year-old who first entered my office and acted so disrespectfully to me had transformed into a woman whose wisdom exceeded her age and who was more than ready to leave home for college. It was as ideal an outcome as either of us could have hoped for when we began her psychotherapy. Since then, I've made it a practice to begin therapy by visualizing its ideal outcome.

Create Your Reality

As we now enjoy the final moments of winning our game, let's look forward together. If things were to work out ideally for your child and for your family, what would that look like? Can you picture it? What would the day-to-day entail? Notice what you are thinking about. If you are seeing your child being happy all the time, let's take a nod from my former patient and make your vision a little more realistic and much more fulfilling. Think back to chapter 2: You're doing your child a disservice if your goal is for her to be constantly comfortable, stimulated, and entertained. That's not the end goal. Imagine your child truly *content*, knowing that indeed, whatever circumstances she encounters while living in reality–the joy, the gratitude, the awkward moments, the losses–it's all good . . . it's all real.

Notice that when you set about visualizing how you want things to look, the natural human tendency is for thoughts to deteriorate into what's not going well and how you *don't* want things to look. Visualizing the very outcome you don't want is the same as worrying! So stay mindful of the specifics of what you're envisioning. Notice also whether you have become distracted entirely. As often as necessary, return your focus to how you want things to be. Keep it real. Paint that picture over and over again. Take slow, deep, diaphragmatic breaths, like an opera singer or yoga instructor. Your visualization has now become a form of mindfulness meditation.

As you visualize, imagine what it will look like when the hard work is over. You aligned your approach with that of your partner. You selected your words with intention, and they now have become permanent objects within your daughter's mind, motivating her in every endeavor. You repainted her room together and recolored your relationship. You did yoga together and mutually enjoyed every moment you spent doing it, instead of letting her stay fixated on some screen. You helped her find within herself, within nature, and within her attachment to you a less intense but longer-lasting kind of stimulation than any screen could offer anyway. Picture your daughter fluidly demonstrating an appreciation of these memories throughout her day, just as you modeled appreciation for her by watching her play in her soccer game instead of watching your tablet. See the way you want it all to look. It's all good.

Imagine your daughter getting promptly dressed for school on her own because she knows how to manage her time without getting sucked in by social media before the day even begins. See her demonstrate what it truly means to stay "tuned in" by how she pays attention even when the teacher lectures for the entire class period. Instead of feeling entitled to technology and indiscriminately pulling out her phone in the middle of class, your daughter treats electronics as the stimulants they are, intentionally directing her focus to the accompanying visual aids when she needs a little tech to help her stay engaged. She chooses to strive for the superordinate reward of the high grade in the class over the immediate but temporary reward of confirming a text came through. As a result of her hard work, see her valiantly outline an answer to the tough essay on the college application, then see her try to contain the confident smile that spreads across her face as she composes with ease. She doesn't punish her mistakes with self-criticism, only to ultimately seek solace in front of a screen. She's made positive self-talk her habit.

Visualize your son reacting calmly when the

football coach gives him tough feedback. He knows the two marshmallows of continuing to play hard and keeping his starting position will be more filling than the one marshmallow of telling his coach off and retreating to his room to play fantasy football. Envision him pushing through fatigue to complete the last five math problems on his homework assignment. He knows how to spend time now to save more time later. He's tired, but he knows that if he finishes strong now, he can go to the movie tomorrow. And, longer-term, he's starting to sense that it's prioritizing his studies in this way today that will take him to the Ivy League tomorrow. Even if the SAT scores aren't quite what he hoped for, see him coming home and choosing to talk out his feelings with you because he trusts you, instead of spraying you with friendly fire. Imagine him on his own, speaking as confidently with his college professors as he does when he calls for pizza, just like you taught him.

How does he do it? He grasps that his true character is bigger than even the Game. He respects that there are natural limits but that he's going to seize every reward he can. He understands that therein lies the true level of control available to him; his now-archaic video game controller only powered a virtual world. He "gets it" and is pleased to know that what he makes of the real world will come more from the development of his person than the dexterity of his fingers. He knows that the castle he someday inhabits will be made of brick and mortar, not graphics . . . that his princess will be one of flesh and bone, not pixels. He recognizes that the rewards he wants the most come through relationships—real relationships like the one you've cultivated with him over hot chocolate or at the record store and the burger joint and the ballpark.

Realize Your Creation

Hey! Is that your daughter—the one with the covers over her head whom her roommate can't wake up this morning? Did she stay awake all night sexting with her boyfriend?

Nah. What I see is that my daughter's already at class. In fact, I know that's where she is because she Instagrammed a beautiful photo this morning of the first snow that fell last night and covered the trees outside her dorm. Yes, she uses technology. But it's most certainly she *who uses it. I can visualize her at swim practice later today. She only has to keep Bs to maintain her swim scholarship, but she's getting As because she chose a major that she truly enjoys.*

Hey! Is that your son—the one stumbling around the fraternity house at 2:00 AM looking for someone to join him in playing another video game?

Heck no. My son's in his room, studying. Sure, he'll play some video games while he's home over winter break. But then next spring, I can imagine him reaping the fruits of his labor, standing proudly on the stage at his fraternity's alumni banquet to receive his merit certificate. He's standing up tall, like a tower that doesn't need any scaffolding.

As you complete your visualization exercise, you might also try imagining the graphs and figures we've used. Imagine what they'll look like when they reflect peace in your home. They will depict high degrees of responsibility in front of high degrees of privilege, and the branch leading to reward will bear so much fruit it will only stay intact because it's so strong. As you move from visualizing to noticing how you're feeling, find within you a deep sense of gratitude. You are blessed with the job of shifting your child's practices from spelunking for what ultimately doesn't matter to striving for what does.

As you make this kind of visualization or meditation a practice, some of what you try to envision about your child's future will become cloudy, in part because the digital age constantly invites the invention of new occupations. While the idea of perpetually emerging jobs can be exciting, it also renders it difficult to see exactly where our kids are headed. And with new jobs come new impacts on the economy and the individual family. You might be one of the many parents balancing more than one job, maybe even more than one career. So how do we prepare our kids for the multiple jobs they might someday possess—especially when some of these roles don't even exist yet?

Lately I have been trying to balance three jobs: husband/father, psychologist, and author. I am writing this chapter on my day "off," and ironically my own daughter is playing by herself. She's not on an electronic device at the moment, but she certainly knows how to use them (and in some ways, better than I do). The point isn't what she's doing right now, but what we're *not* doing together while I'm the only adult at home this afternoon. I believe it's part of my life's purpose to finish this book, but in turn, the aim of the book is to encourage us all to reestablish authentic connections with one another.

I find myself recalling one of the final episodes

of *Mad Men*, in which two adolescent characters opt for looking through a telescope at the moon instead of watching the Apollo moon landing on TV. One says to the other, "Isn't that *so* much better than TV?" You want Junior to shoot for the moon. That starts with orienting him to the actual moon.

Let's do it. Now.

Seriously, what if we both set this book aside for a moment before finishing it? I'll quit typing and go squeeze my daughter. I'll tell her how special she is to me, and I'll invite her to play the off-screen game of her choice. Might you mark your place in the book and invite your child to do the same? If he refuses an off-screen game, could you go on a walk? If you're thinking, *But it's cold outside*, then even better. Bundle up and enjoy the stimulation of the brisk air. Neither of you will forget this totally spontaneous hike.

★ ★ ★

What did you do? More important, how did it go? If it was a success, pass your story along to your friends and extended family. Tweet it! Make it go viral. My daughter and I assembled a giant floor puzzle, with me positioning the pieces and her snapping them into place. I was aiming to provide scaffolding, but then I really *became* scaffolding when she started climbing on me, which is something we both love. We not only connected the pieces with one another, *we* connected with one another. Once the whole puzzle came together, I noticed that the educational toy company Melissa & Doug manufactured it, and that their slogan, also revealed by virtue of the completed picture, nicely balances technology with relationship: "Lights, Camera, Interaction."

Next, what if we both take a nod from the slogan and continue to model for our kids how to use technology to plan unplugged activities, by logging on to sites like redtri.com and letsmove. gov that provide lists of such activities? Or recall the idea from chapter 4 that we can find favorite recipes online and then prepare the meals together with our kids. Or we might start even simpler, and just scramble some eggs for sit-down breakfasts early tomorrow morning, nourishing our kids—via the object permanence of the shared meal more than the sustenance of the food—for adventures in reality: surfing waves with friends at the beach . . . serving meals to strangers at the shelter . . . navigating a ropes course . . . navigating an academic course . . . strolling with grandparents through the county fair . . . finally beating us at one-on-one in the driveway. These adventures do not calibrate the Minecraft compass, but the moral compass. It's the one that shows where our kids are headed, so calibrating it is how we prepare them for the future. Tweet *that*.

You've Really Let Yourself Mii Go

We just won our game! But finishing this book is only the beginning of your next adventure. As Mario establishes after conquering each level, your princess or prince still awaits your rescue. From here, the stakes remain staggeringly high, and playing will require many of your faculties. You will need your instincts, and wisdom that overmatches strength. You will rely on your measurement of what's happening and how it's going over time. You will call upon what you have learned about how kids learn. You will need to know when to implement the Triangle Defense. You won't always know exactly what to say, but you'll know what *not* to say. You will need to dole out not punishment, but reward. You will need to demonstrate not perfection, but integrity. You aren't the problem, and neither is your kid. Because you are integral to the solution, you must take care of yourself in order to clean your fishbowl.

Your completing this book has equipped

you with all you will need in order to unplug and reconnect. With all the tech-free activities you've started doing with your kid, you're getting into phenomenal shape (though your Mii looks neglected).

Time to reward yourself. Maybe you should invite some friends over, tell them to bring their inner children, and call for pizza.

Acknowledgments

I cannot begin to express how deep my gratitude runs for so very many people in my life. Each of you has somehow shaped this book. To my soul mate, Carrie . . . to our joys Ashton and her brother-to-be . . . to my parents and brother . . . to my in-laws and extended family . . . to my therapist and my editors . . . to my mentors, colleagues, clients, and close friends: As I pursue my life's passion every day, I am humbled to pass along the energy you have passed to me. Thank you.

References

Bajovic, M. "Violent video gaming and moral reasoning in adolescents: is there an association?" *Educational Media International* 50 (2013), 177-91.

Bandura, A., D. Ross, and S. A. Ross. "Transmission of aggression through imitation of aggressive models." *Journal of Abnormal and Social Psychology* 63 (1961), 575-82.

Granic, I., A. Lobel, and R. C. M. E. Engels. "The benefits of playing video games." *American Psychologist* 69 (2014), 66-78.

Kinney, J. *Diary of a Wimpy Kid: Cabin Fever*. New York: Abrams, 2011: 47.

Kuhn, S., T. Gleich, R. C. Lorenz, U. Lindenberger, and J. Gallinat. "Playing Super Mario induces structural brain plasticity: gray matter changes resulting from training with a commercial video game." *Molecular Psychiatry* 19 (2014), 265-71.

Mischel, W. and E. B. Ebbesen. "Attention in delay of gratification." *Journal of Personality and Social Psychology* 16 (1970): 329-37.

Mitchell, S. A. and M. J. Black. *Freud and Beyond: A History of Modern Psychoanalytic Thought.* New York: Basic Books, 1995: 55.

Thompson, D. "'Electronic cocaine': A new look at addiction to computers." *The Telegraph* (2014), online publication, http://blogs. telegraph.co.uk, accessed May 21, 2014.

Index

About the Author

D r. Joe Dilley's passion has always been psychology. He first became interested in the field when he was a boy, through dinnertime discussions with his father, a clinical psychologist, and his mother, a former special education teacher. He began officially pursuing his life's work at the University of Iowa, where he graduated with honors in psychology and a double minor in religion and philosophy. Joe then brought a multifaceted view of the human psyche to his doctoral studies at Northwestern University in downtown Chicago. There, he completed his PhD in clinical psychology, specializing in strengths-based therapy for children, teens, and adults.

Dr. Joe Dilley is now a licensed clinical psychologist and the cofounder of Synergy Psychological, the private practice he started in 2009 with his wife, Dr. Carrie Dilley. Synergy is nestled in the quaint foothill village of Sierra Madre, just outside Pasadena, California. The

Dilleys chose the name Synergy to reflect the complementary ways in which the mind, body, and spirit interact within a healthy individual or family, as well as to highlight the collaborative nature of therapy itself. Outside of their practice, the Dilleys most enjoy long days of "active relaxation" with their daughter, Ashton, as they anticipate the impending arrival of their son.

GAME OVER

.